More Appreciation

for author Gordie White

After many trips abroad and four decades in the outdoors, I was amazed at how much I learned reading *Field Notes from Wild Places*. Gordie White has done a masterful job crafting interesting, exciting, compelling, and detailed vicarious journeys for the reader. *Field Notes from Wild Places* now holds the spot as the best of the many hunting book I have ever read.

— **Michael Dorn,** Author
Staying Alive—How to Act Fast and Survive Deadly Encounters

Gordie is the most modest hunter I know, yet his stories are as rich, entertaining, and action-packed as anything by Ruark, Hemingway, or Corbett. How does he do that? He's just that damn good of a writer.

— **Gayne C. Young,** Editor, *North American Hunter*
and author of *And Monkeys Threw Crap at Me*
and *Adventures in Hunting, Fishing, and Writing*

For Randy & Mickey,

I wrote this book for my family and friends. Here is your copy. Thank you for taking great care of my friends and clients.

Your Friend,

Mollie White

Feb 2018

FIELD NOTES *from* WILD PLACES

GORDIE WHITE

Publisher's Cataloging-in-Publication Data
• Hunting— 2.Wild Life—3.—Memoir
PS

ISBN: 978-0-9981265-0-0

Library of Congress Control Number:

Editor-in-Chief—Mindy Reed, The Authors' Assistant
Cover Design and Creative—Rebecca Byrd Arthur

Printed in the United States of America

For My Family

Table of Contents

FOREWORD

by Berit Aagaard

Sometime in 1996 an old friend, Col. Dennis Behrens, who had hunted with us during our Kenya days, came to visit us, bringing with him a young man to see Finn. Finn, my late husband was a longtime professional hunter in Kenya until all legal hunting was abruptly banned in 1977. The young man was obviously quite nervous and the Colonel felt the two should meet because he knew both men well and that they had a lot in common.

Finn wrote journals of every hunt he had done, both private and professional, and kept meticulous records of every round fired from any rifle he shot. These journals and records became invaluable to Finn as he started writing for magazines such as *American Hunter* and *American Rifleman* and many others. They not only contained technical information, but detailed accounts of innumerable hunts.

As they were introduced and started talking, our anxious young man, Gordie White, hung on every word Finn spoke, and he admired the journals, and handled them with reverence. He had read every article of Finn's that he could get his hands on, and felt Finn had been his mentor, and idol, when it came to hunting dangerous game. (Much later he admitted to being desperately nervous because he knew how famous Finn had become, and had tremendous respect and admiration for him.) The two quickly connected and the conversation soon flowed easily.

It was fascinating to listen to these two men, both avid hunters, but from such different beginnings and backgrounds. Finn was born in Kenya and had hunted there all his life; Gordie's early experience was shooting "partridge" with his dad in Canada. Later, he had followed his life-long dream of hunting professionally. He had recently returned from hunting in Zimbabwe and credited Finn with giving him the incentive and courage to pursue that dream.

I could identify with Gordie. Finn had given me courage and incentive as well. Shortly after we were married, I took out on my first professional photographic safari where we hunted with cameras instead of guns. His enthusiasm and encouragement made me believe I could do it. I had always enjoyed hiking in the woods of my native Norway, using all my senses while exploring, but the African bush was so different and there were so many more things to learn and discover. I quickly realized that it was up to me to find the game and help my clients to open their eyes and see, make them aware of their surroundings and experience the "magic" of the African bush. It was a joy for me when it was a client who spotted game or remarked on something unusual. Of course there were lions and elephants, rhino and buffalo, but there were also spectacular sunsets, thousands of birds, the little DikDik defending his territory around a mound of his tiny droppings, or the crazy wildebeest that never could quite decide which direction to run. Finn invited me to add my comments to his journals and they also became valuable memories of happenings that otherwise would be forgotten.

Like Finn, Gordie has kept field notes just like we did, and now they are coming into their own; they have been expanded and are ready to be shared. It is always a challenge to find the best words that describe what you are trying to relay to others, whether painting a picture of beautiful scenery, sharing emotions, or telling about something dramatic. There may be a searching for words and a struggle to use them well, but when it all comes together so that the reader can "see" through your words, then you have "arrived." That is your reward.

Here are stories that very much demonstrate both the love for and the understanding of things wild. Anyone who has ever experienced the thrill of the hunt, the satisfaction of achieving a personal goal, whether it is photographing a butterfly at rest, (which can be a real challenge by the way), or downing a charging elephant only a few paces from disaster, will identify themselves in these stories written with honesty, love, and understanding—and will recall adventures of their own. They may even be encouraged to write some of their own special tales for posterity.

Gordie has captured the art of storytelling, word sparing, with emotion and warmth. From brief field notes, he shares with us the wonders and beauty of the wild; the excitement and lessons learned, the gratitude to be alive. There is no bravado here, the stories are told with honesty and humor—never trying to exaggerate or make a situation more fantastic than it really was. His adventures don't need exaggeration; they were quite exciting enough without any help. He has grasped the essence of the famous quote: "We do not hunt to kill; we kill to have hunted." When Finn presented Gordie with a copy of his book Aagaard's Africa: A Hunter Remembers he wrote the dedication: "To Gordon White, a fellow African hunter, who has been there and seen the elephant, and loved it."

No Turning Back

I'd stripped down to my full-length, bright red long underwear and wool socks. I was sitting in the saddle on a tall black horse—we were near the water's edge of a lake in the Yukon Territory. My focus was on the cabin across the inlet. It stood close to the shoreline, on a hillside, surrounded by alders and a few spruce trees. The remaining daylight was fading quickly on this wintry gray October day. The horse was jittery: nervously stepping backwards and sideways while I heeled his flank to press on forward. John O'Brien, my hunting client from California, stood behind me and next to my piled-up gear: daypack, jacket, pants, and boots. We'd been on horseback all day, venturing above timberline, looking for a Dall ram or a grizzly. We didn't see either one. Since daybreak, the warming sun had never materialized. I felt raw. My bones ached.

Gloveless, my hands were cold and bloodless as I pinched leather reins between a thumb and forefinger. I noticed ice crystals on the sand at the water's edge. The big gelding stepped into the dark lake, splashing in the shallows. I kicked him hard; he moved into deeper water. For several strides, he had good footing while the water climbed his legs to his barrel chest and over my feet and calves. He kept going. The water was frigid, almost electrifying. I kept driving my heels into him until the moment I felt us float, like moving through the air. He no longer had the lake bottom for traction. Water began to crest his back and rise above my waist. It was time to get off. I slid leftward from my saddle and with my right hand, I gripped the saddle horn. I counted on the horse to take me across to the far shoreline—I'd done it before—but this time it was a bitter arctic plunge. The gelding swam a short distance, and then decided to abort the crossing. He turned back towards the shore. As the black horse arched to the right, I let go of the horn and began to swim with everything I had. It was vital I get across the channel of water.

While I stroked and kicked ferociously, the icy water brought extreme pain to my chest. I felt as though my ribcage was being crushed in a giant vice. I could hardly breathe. I heard John shouting from the bank, but I didn't hear words, it was just noise.

I was getting across the inlet, but the numbing of my legs and arms, and the tightening of my chest intensified. My pace became slower and slower…and then…I stopped. I couldn't swing another stroke. I locked up. My mind raced. Intense fear set in—I thought I was about to drown. The brushy shoreline was maybe a hundred feet away, and I clearly saw the skinny, dirt path that climbed the slope to the cabin. I was so close. My legs dropped down, my body became vertical, and I began to sink. As my head dropped below the surface, I quickly felt my feet touch the soft mud bottom. I took a few steps, and my head was out of the water. The fear of drowning was gone. I walked the short distance to the lake's edge, stepped up on the bank, turned back, and looked towards John. I threw my right arm up and waved.

Within a few minutes, the cabin's wood stove roared with fire, throwing much-needed heat. I was numb all over and shaking uncontrollably. I was lucky.

Yukon Territory
October 6, 1994

We saw a cow and a calf moose, and one nice 60 inch bull up in sheep country.... I had to swim in front of camp yesterday. It was really bloody cold.... The swim was about 75 yards...

Growing up, there were always guns around. My father taught me to shoot and hunt, paddle a canoe, and fish. He showed me how to read topographical maps and use a compass. To this day, I've never been lost in the woods. He taught me to respect and appreciate animals, forests, rivers, lakes, and fish. He pressed ethics upon me. I grew up hunting and fishing—lived a life in the woods and on the water. Hunting was not pastime or recreation. It was not something you chose to do or not do. It was part of our lives. It was something we did and understood.

As a kid, I started reading every outdoor book and magazine I could get my hands on. The writers were my heroes. They flooded my life with stories of hair-raising adventures of exotic and distant places. These luminaries hunted dangerous game: elephant, lion, buffalo, big bears; they climbed peaks for sheep, deer, and elk; and they stalked herds of antelope on the African plains. These writers, later, became my mentors. I wanted to write, too, and I did. I kept a journal of the places I visited and the game I hunted. I chronicled the guns and cartridges used and their performance in the field. I kept detailed records. Today, my notes remind me that I spent many days in solitude, but they also call to attention the people who joined me afield: family, friends, guides, professional hunters, and clients. I've written hundreds of pages, and I've never shared them with anyone.

For those who hunt, there is an acute awareness and purpose to pursue birds and big game on the prairie and in the timber. There is meaning to the chase of wild things. This book is about rediscovery, people, animals, and places far-off and closer to home.

And, ultimately, it's about sharing some of my experiences.

Shooting Partridge

October 16, 1988

Got up at 11 A.M. Went on Lariviere's trail and shot bird near Pike Lake. Shot a partridge near Simpson and one near the dam. Saw 5 deer, 1 buck and 4 does. Missed 3 birds today. Nice day, last day of hunting this time. Total for this trip: 4 partridge, saw 9 deer. This season to date I've seen 21 deer and about 40 partridge.

I remember the first time I saw my father kill a ruffed grouse. I was a young boy, perhaps eight years old. It was an unusually warm September day. Dad drove his company-issued baby blue Monte Carlo. The sunshine shimmered through the back windshield of the car. My grandfather, grandmother, father, mother, my brother Mike, and I filled the car to total discomfort. The car was packed tight, and I recall being miserable. The road was dusty; rocks flew as we vibrated along the gravel road somewhere in the

17

Laurentian Mountains of Southern Quebec. A family friend's lake-front cottage was the destination. I was tired of being in the car, and I wanted the drive to end.

Without warning, my father brought the sedan to an abrupt halt and stepped out. He'd spotted a ruffed grouse, what we always referred to as "partridge." Dad walked around to the rear of the car; opened the trunk, and retrieved his blaze-orange vest and cap, put them on like it was military dress. He slid his .410 from its case, loaded the slim single-shot, and walked to the front of the car. He shot the ground-level grouse a short distance away in short weeds that were a few feet from the edge of the gravel road. Now the bird wasn't in flight. It had been walkin'—ever so slowly—across the dirt road. Dad performed the act with purpose and serious intent. The White family looked on unapologetically with little expression: as if this was all perfectly normal.

My mother likely said, "Well done, Bob" or something to that effect, and if she did, he'd of replied, "Merci, Angele."

My father put the grouse in a cardboard box with flaps folded inward to prevent the dying bird from escaping, and placed the .410 back in its case. He removed his vest and hat, and returned all to the trunk. It was a legal kill…I think.

He got back into the car and we were once again moving down the dusty road while the grouse violently kicked, flapped, and fluttered its nerves out in the box. A short while later, the audible thrashing ended and the bird was still.

The twentieth century Spanish philosopher, Jose Ortega y Gasset, once wrote: "One does not hunt in order to kill, but to kill in order to have hunted." I don't think he had my father in mind when he penned that phrase. Dad did in fact kill, but I believe there was no hunting involved. The bird died from bad timing and a drive-by shooting.

I remember my dad's annual partridge hunting expeditions with his buddy Jack Delmar who had emigrated from Holland. I recall Mr. Delmar could hardly speak any English, but that did not seem to matter. Each season my father's dust-covered company sedan rolled into the driveway, Mr. Delmar riding shotgun, to be greeted by Mom, Mike and I. We anxiously wanted to see what lay in the bottom of Dad's tan-colored canvas hunting bag. Typically, there was a half dozen or so grouse, occasionally, there was a snowshoe hare, and once there was a dead marten mixed in with the birds.

Dad and Mr. Delmar, unshaven and rank, stood near Mike and me smiling, tired, and glad to be home. I was eager to hear about their hunt. I wanted to know if they saw deer, moose, and maybe, a bear. I pestered Dad for all the details. A photo session would soon follow. As I flipped through old photo albums, the faded photos from my father's annual trips looked similar: Mike and I standing on our front lawn, holding a slender pole between us at shoulder height, grouse hung string-tied by their necks, causing it to sag. But we posed proudly with dead birds, and dreamed that one day, we too would hunt grouse.

I have a vivid memory of a grouse hunt with my father when I was still very young. We were in a typical eastern Canadian boreal forest of towering spruce and birch trees. During the prime days of grouse season, the leaves are constantly changing colors and intermittently drift and fall. The smells of the damp soil and leaf mold underfoot are fresh and invigorate the senses. Dad carried his favorite .410, and I walked beside him carrying a plastic AR-15— a toy model that made an obnoxious grinding sound when the trigger was squeezed.

———————————

Another trip took place in the fall of 1980. Our hunting party included Dad, my brother, Mike, my older cousin, Maurice, and his five-year-old son (my second cousin), Dominic, and my best friend, Johnny Weightman. Maurice owned a cabin in grouse country and would serve as our guide. This would be my first time to shoot wild game.

We left Montreal in Maurice's old blue Chevy pickup. Mike, Johnny, Dominic, and I rode in the covered truck bed with all the gear: food, milk, beer, wine, and guns. We ran our mouths, wrestled tirelessly, and were giddy with anticipation of the hunt ahead. After what seemed to us an eternity of driving on highways and then logging roads, we finally reached our hunting camp: Michomis, an old cabin located on the banks on the Gatineau River in Central Quebec.

The cabin, void of any luxuries, was a true deep woods hunting camp with a high mouse population, a fire hazard woodstove, and a long-drop outhouse twenty steps from the front door. I don't remember getting unpacked, settled in, or what I ate for dinner, but

Shooting Partridge

I do recall lying in bed anxious to fall asleep. I wanted the night to end so I could wake up and begin my first partridge hunt.

When I woke up, I had little patience for the morning routine—I was about to go on my first hunt with a loaded shotgun—I wanted to get going. Just as we finished breakfast and were about to leave camp, Johnny looked out the window and saw a big grouse slowly high-stepping across the truck path that led to the cabin. Because Johnny spotted the grouse first, he got first shot. We told Dad of the sighting, shotguns were uncased, and we scurried out of the back door of the shack. We snuck around the side of the cabin until we could see the grouse in the two-track road. We stalked, crept, and sneaked within range. Johnny cocked the hammers back on our family's antique Stevens 12 gauge side-by-side, took careful aim, and ground-sluiced the bird. The first grouse of the trip died. It was a large specimen and we repeatedly commented on the size of its pronounced breast. For Johnny, Mike, and me, the hunt started well on that glorious morning.

The remainder of that day, and the next two, we drove around, scanning the area, and walked along abandoned brush trails, searching for grouse. The ruffed grouse, like their upland cousins, prefer edge cover for movement and existence. Grouse can be easily spotted *graveling*—nibbling small stones that assist the gizzard with digestion. That's why driving old logging and gravel roads is an effective technique for hunters who simply want to find and kill grouse rather than hunt the grand bird with a trained bird dog and shoot over a productive point. Once a solitary bird or small group—two to three—is spotted, the driver is alerted, and the vehicle comes to a halt. The hunter steps out, loads the shotgun, and begins to stalk with quiet finesse to within a suitable killing distance of 25 yards or so. As the wonderful drummer of the woods stands there, immobile, the hunter squeezes the trigger and slays the bird. If a mate is close enough, a portion of the pellet pattern may hit that bird too, so a double kill is achieved with a single discharge.

We shot and retrieved numerous ruffed grouse, one spruce grouse, and a single snowshoe hare, but it was a spruce grouse that caused drama during that inaugural hunt. Mike saw a partridge flush up unto a low-lying branch, cocked the hammer back on his .410, took careful aim, and shot the bird from its perch. This red crested partridge tumbled to the ground, flopped in its death throes, and within moments came to a rest. Ten-year-old Mike went over, picked up the pretty grouse, paused, gazed and gasped when he saw entrails spill out from its chest cavity. The experience unsettled him and he began to cry. While Mike's spirit was utterly broken, I thought the trip to Michomis was a great adventure—the beginning of my lifelong pursuit of upland birds.

In 1981, our family joined the Kensington Fish and Game Club, a private enterprise that operated and managed a massive tract of crown land east of Maniwaki—a small logging town on the banks of the Gatineau River. Within the club's boundaries, we had access to 20 or more lakes and thousands of acres of boreal forest. At Kensington, my dad hunted deer with the "old-timers,"

Shooting Partridge

a dozen or so senior club members who annually hunted the first week of the provincial rifle deer season. I couldn't hunt with the men because I wasn't old enough—you had to be sixteen years old to join the hunting party during the regular rifle season. However, I was allowed to hunt grouse, snowshoe hare, and deer with a bow. The club had whitetails, but not many by the standards seen in the Southern U.S. or on the South Texas ranches I came to manage years later. We fished too. The club's lakes had speckled, rainbow, and grey trout, as well as big northern pike.

Prior to the deer season's opening weekend, the first two weeks of November, my parents took Mike and me to Kensington to hunt grouse on weekends. The club had countless miles of walking trails and grown-over logging roads, which was perfect country to hunt grouse. From our cabin, we accessed many miles of trails and walked all day; or we'd get in a boat, cross the lake, tie up at a trailhead and walk until we could no longer walk. I recall the days I hiked in the forest with Dad and Mike—where I'd hear the grouse drum and to see whitetail deer bounding away—the woods were wild.

One overcast October day, Dad and I walked a familiar trail lined with birch and a scattering of spruce. We spotted a grouse as it entered the trail ahead of us. The bird was within shooting distance. Dad said, "Go ahead and take him."

I cocked the hammer on my .410, and took a few hurried steps towards the grouse—it flushed. I then took a quick snap shot before the bird was lost behind cover.

Dad exclaimed, "Why didn't you just shoot it on the ground?" I responded, "I think I got the partridge, Dad."

I was confident I saw the bird tumble, but my father was unsure and not pleased. We walked over and found the grouse—dead, lying in the leaves. It was my first bird ever taken on the wing and I felt sense of accomplishment. Once again, Dad queried why I chose to shoot the grouse flying and I informed him, "Dad, the Americans shoot their birds flying!" I took another grouse flying the following day, with a single-shot 16 gauge. We looked hard to find the downed bird, but recovered it and placed in the tan canvas bag.

During my college years, I lived, breathed, and slept hunting. I read every book and magazine I could afford to buy, and wanted nothing more than to be in the woods with my shotgun, rifle, or bow. A few weekends during the hunting season, I loaded my Mazda pickup—a delightfully aged dark blue B2000 model with a "new" black front quarter panel, replacing the deteriorated rusted-out original, very bald tires, and a .223 bullet hole through the side of the bed from a woodchuck hunt mishap. With gear, guns, clothes, food, and a tank full of gas, I headed north for Kensington. The four-hour drive took me around gentle mountains, through valleys, and along the edges of fresh water lakes bordered with cozy cottages.

I traveled just before sunset and took in the spectacular colors of fall foliage revealed on the mountains. Along the way, I stopped at francophone villages and towns such as: Labelle, Lac-des-Ecorces, and Mt. Laurier, to buy last minute essentials: milk, bread, Cokes, chocolate chip cookies, and more fuel. The convenience stores—

Shooting Partridge

depanneurs—were small, privately owned enterprises that generated sales mainly from selling beer, ice, and cigarettes. The French-speaking proprietors routinely asked if I was hunting for the locals' favorite game animal: *l'orignal.* My reply was that I wasn't after moose but hoped to find *perdrix* (partridge). I paid for my sundries, said *merci,* and was bid farewell with *bonne chance et bonne chasse.*

The last stretch of road was thirty lonely miles of gravel road and dark forests. The truck came to a stop with headlights shining on the brown log cabin. My lakeside quarters were heated by a woodstove. I carried drinking water by bucket from the shore to the kitchen, and when darkness fell, I ate and read by oil lamp and candles. There was no shower or plumbing, but an outhouse stood in the timber a dozen or so steps behind the cabin. I always found great comfort in my simple cabin—it was paradise.

Mornings were fresh and crisp, so leaving the comfort of my sleeping bag was a challenge. Breakfast was a bowl of cereal or a peanut butter and jelly sandwich complimented with a tall glass of milk. Soon after filling my stomach, I was out the door in full upland attire, my shotgun cradled. I'd either walk trails from camp or I might decide to boat across the lake to a trailhead. For a couple or three days, I meandered the in the woods in search of grouse or I sat high in a tree to ambush a whitetail in bow range. It was always a time of quiet solitude. When I wasn't hunting, I wrote in my journal, and read books by Ruark, McGuane, Harrison, and Hemingway.

Whenever I went out on these excursions, I routinely managed to bring home at least half a dozen grouse. I remember I once stalked a small doe in misting rain and took her with my bow. These solo trips were formative experiences that transformed hunting into a passion and later my vocation.

ALBERTA
October 15, 1997

Lino and I got one hour of grouse hunting in. He missed one, we then walked through some good cover and flushed two, and we each killed a bird. Col. Behrens and Col. Brown fly in tomorrow—we are going for ducks and geese.

The ruffed grouse population is cyclical in nature with population highs occurring approximately every ten years. In the peak cycles, I enjoyed excellent hunting in central Quebec, but it was years later, in Alberta, that I found much higher concentrations of grouse.

I worked as a big game guide in the Peace River country of northern Alberta and I spent many hours scouting for trophy whitetails, mule deer, elk, and moose. I walked, hiked, and drove through endless agricultural country, logging cutovers, and spruce and aspen forests. The reconnaissance missions provided countless grouse sightings when looking for sign of bucks and bulls, but I rarely carried a shotgun while working in the Peace Country. I guided hunters nearly every day of the season and

Shooting Partridge

wouldn't dare fire a shot at grouse in areas that held trophy game, fearing a shot fired would scare deer, elk, and moose, causing the game to leave the area.

In October 1997, my parents came to Alberta to visit Mike and me. My brother was guiding for the same outfitter but was hunting from a camp west of my guiding area. I drove to Mike's camp, a trashy and confusing maze of attached, dated, dark, and dingy single-wide trailers, located on a quiet street in a tiny farming community. Our good friend from Montreal, Lino Pettinichi, was in camp as chef, mallard caller, *raconteur,* bird cleaner, and hunting buddy.

One morning, Mike took Dad deer hunting in the Birch Hills, a gentle mountain range bordering vast farm fields of alfalfa and wheat, while Lino and I decided to go grouse hunting at a nearby conservation area that had miles of walking trails and perfect bird habitat. Within an hour of hiking through the poplar and spruce forests, several grouse were found: a few missed and a brace taken. The birds were placed in the tan canvas hunting bag. Mike killed a whitetail buck that day too. It should have been Dad who took the deer…but that is another story.

The next time our family was together, we were in an intensive -care hospital room in Montreal, anxiously waiting for a donor liver to arrive and save my mother's life. It arrived, but ultimately, too late. My mother died on Thanksgiving Day in 1998.

Every day I hunted with Dad, he carried *the* canvas hunting bag slung over one shoulder. For more than 30 hunting seasons, it held countless partridge, hares, a map, compass, matches, sandwiches, sodas, and hard candies. The bag is now retired, in Texas, and hangs on a wall in my office.

At this writing, I have not been back to either the hunting grounds of my youth or Alberta to pursue the explosive flushing ruffed grouse. Someday, I plan to return to either or both. It is unlikely that Dad, Mike, or I (together) will ever walk the endless trails and familiar haunts of Kensington to hunt for partridge.

I miss hunting with Dad and Mike.

And There Were Elephants

ZIMBABWE

April 19, 1995

> *The council requested 1 cow elephant and 3 impala for April 17...I parked at the top of the escarpment. We immediately saw elephant. 1 herd of about 50 and a herd of 5 closer to our ridge...I got within 15 yards and the wind started shifting...I shot her from 12 yards, she went down, I went closer, she got up facing me, I shot her again...She died on her knees...*

I remember being very anxious. April 18 is Independence Day in Zimbabwe and the local tribal council wanted an elephant cow and three impala for their evening festivities. The meat had to be delivered before nightfall.

It was the evening of April 16 and I had to shoot an elephant and have it skinned, quartered, de-boned, and loaded in the Toyota Land Cruisers by noon the following day. This was major pressure and I was stressed.

It was my second season in Zimbabwe and I had been in the country for three weeks. I had spent time hunting elephant the previous season. I scouted for big bulls for upcoming safaris, filmed clients hunting trophy tuskers, chased dozens of crop raiding elephants from maize fields, but I hadn't shot my first elephant. My opportunity arrived and I was on a very tight schedule.

An hour before sunrise, and after a sleepless night, my tracker Albert, and government game scout, Pension, and I climbed into the Toyota and headed down the two-track road that led out of camp. A dozen men were loaded in two additional Toyotas and followed us. The extra men were skinners and locals there to assist with the butchering of the animal…if one was taken.

We arrived at a ridge that overlooked a dry riverbed that snaked through favored elephant habitat just as the sun rose over the hills of the rugged Zambezi Valley. I'd seen herds of elephant in this valley many times before. The previous evening, I'd found plenty of impala, so shooting three for the council was a simple affair; but now, I had to find a mature cow early enough in the day, shoot her, and have the meat delivered for the evening's grand festivities. Failure to deliver the elephant meat would mean not fulfilling my obligation to the council…a calamity I did not want to face.

As the sun gave more light to the valley below, Albert was first to spot two herds of elephants—as he often did without the use of binoculars. The larger herd of fifty or so animals ranged from newborn calves to old tired bulls. The closer herd had five elephants: three cows and a couple of youngsters. It was a perfect

And There Were Elephants

group to stalk. I dropped down off the ridge and chambered a 500 grain FMJ into my battered .458 Winchester Mag.

We started towards the small group and slowly made our way down the steep slope, trying our best not to slip, fall, or tumble. We reached flatter ground where we could appreciate the idyllic morning breeze that engulfed us in gentle gusts from where the elephants stood. Albert led us through the chest-high vegetation, picking the quietest route, while I kept my eyes on the elephants. Pension followed. We carefully tiptoed around thorny limbs and strategically placed our feet on clear sand, in an attempt to minimize the chance of breaking a small stick or crushing dry leaves underfoot. Elephants have tremendous hearing abilities; any noise from us would have them stampeding for parts unknown.

The elephant moved from our left to right and were oblivious to our presence. It was going well. We angled right, hoping to cut them off before they reached the much thicker riverine along the dry river, and kept moving closer. The small group was now twenty-five or so paces away and still moving slowly to our right. I signaled Albert and Pension to pull up while I stalked in closer to shoot. I'd picked out a mature cow that was last in line. Twenty-five paces is close, but the vegetation was blocking most of the elephant—I had to get closer for any chance for a clear shot. I clearly remember on my final few steps that my hands began to sweat profusely! I wiped them on my olive-colored shorts, which made no difference.

Moderate to high panic set in, my heart began to race and my temples throbbed. I pressed on and stalked closer and closer. At twelve paces (later measured), I'd reached the limits of the stalk. The band of elephants grew nervous. Discerned, they knew something was amiss, and hurried their strides. The cow in the rear spun her head in my direction and quickly turned it back—she was heading out! I sidestepped into a small opening to get an unobstructed view of the cow. I shouldered my rifle, pushed the safety forward, put the front bead slightly behind her front shoulder, and squeezed the trigger.

As the shot rang out, she spun to face me. I ejected the spent shell casing and rammed a fresh round in the chamber. My next shot hit her on the opposite shoulder but quartering towards me. Again, she spun and stumbled. I fired a third shot into her chest. My .458 was empty and the action was open. As I was loading more rounds into the magazine, I kept my eyes on the elephant—she was kneeling and motionless. I quickly scurried up very close to her and fired a final head shot. It was over. I'd killed my first elephant and I did it on my own. The stress was gone and the anxiety eased away. Emotions crashed inside me: pride, elation, and joy. Ever since I was a young kid, back when I was tracking snowshoe hares in powdery snow while carrying a .22 rifle, I would daydream that I was on the spoor of a hundred pounder. But the moment surpassed my wildest dreams. For a few minutes, I admired the cow. I ran my hand along her small simple ivory, and felt her hard grey skin. I then felt regret. Although she was undoubtedly older than me, I knew the killing of an elephant has a dark side.

Albert and Pension were at my side, grinning from ear-to-ear. They told me what a great a hunter I was. I thanked them. Truth is, that every aspect of this hunt actually fell into place perfectly.

And There Were Elephants

The skinners and their helpers heard the shots and immediately began cutting a truck path. The vehicles reached the deceased cow in no time. The skinners, both young and old, surrounded the cow in awe. They extended their hands to congratulate me with their traditional multiple-grip handshake. I received more praise and was told by the team that I was a skilled hunter.

I didn't doubt their sincerity, but knew there was also a motive behind the exaggerated compliments—it was meat. They hoped I'd allow them each a small portion of the fresh meat. I did.

For the next couple of hours, the men with knives and machetes spoke incessantly over one another in their native Tonga while skinning and chopping. When the task of butchering the cow was complete, the only sign of where this majestic animal once stood, then died, was the bloodstained grass. For the protein-deprived African, there is seldom sadness with the death of an elephant.

The elephant and impala meat was delivered on time for the 1995 Independence Day celebration. Hundreds of villagers surrounded the Toyotas, and within minutes, the meat was gone. We drove off. Mission accomplished.

Prior to first arriving to the Zambezi Valley, I was told that the elephants were appallingly overpopulated in the area and were a constant nuisance to the local people and their crops. Before long, after driving many miles through the communal lands, I came to understand the elephant population dynamics. As the native population grew exponentially, it forced the people living there to clear land for new villages, thatched huts, and subsistence farms. These settlements pushed wild animals from their home ranges. Where humans and wild animals collide: problems begin.

During the harvest season, problem animal reports arrived into camp daily. Reports varied: buffalo were eating a farmer's cotton crop, or a leopard killed a Tonga's prized ewe. But the majority of the reports dealt with elephants. Locals grew maize (corn) to grind into the staple food: melee meal or sadza. Everyone knows that circus elephants love peanuts, but the wild elephants love maize even more. In the late afternoons, the grey mammoths would routinely stroll out of the unpeopled game parks, step over a five foot heavy gauge wire fence, and casually meander into the closest maize field for dinner. They'd destroy and eat the standing crop, and worse, pushed over an elevated grain bin that held a season's harvest, spilling a native's entire annual income on the ground. Not good.

While the farmers were busy harvesting the grain, I was equally busy investigating reports of crop damage. I verified recent elephant activity and devised a plan to discourage the elephants from destroying more crops. Once fresh sign was found, Albert and I sat in the shade of a nearby tree on the edge of a planted field and waited. I had two guns: a big-bore rifle and a twelve gauge loaded with lead bird shot. I drank a Coke and ate kudu biltong and fresh bread from the local township bakery. I watched the sun set as eagles and vultures flew high overhead. I often spotted the brilliantly colored lilac-breasted rollers as they fluttered from branch to branch. I watched black-shouldered kites hover in suspension, studying the ground below for an unaware rodent, then dive down and snatch a field mouse in its talons.

Human activity was everywhere: Young boys moved goats, sheep, and cattle from watering holes to brush-lined paddocks. Barefoot women swept debris and loose dirt away from their thatched huts while babies clung to their backs secured with brightly colored shawls. Chickens ranged freely, and tan colored dogs paced slowly, but rarely barked. Donkeys with long floppy ears stood motionless and appeared bored with life. Men in frayed shorts, threadbare t-shirts, and sandals made of rubber tread from tires came to the tree for a visit where we'd exchange pleasantries in Fanagalo.

With the black African night thirty minutes away, single or multiple massive grey forms started to appear and enter the maize fields. My goal was to prevent crop destruction and persuade the elephants to return to their daytime haven.

Elephants have comparatively poor eyesight and can be easily approached with favorable wind direction and a quiet stalk. The ideal range is thirty to fifty yards—any closer can risk a charge with deadly intent. At the moment I decided to pepper the elephant(s), I'd swap guns with Albert, and give him my .458 or .500 and replace it with the twelve gauge. I immediately began to send birdshot into the rear ends of the marauding invaders. The elephants' heavy hide easily deflected the tiny lead pellets. No physical harm done, just short-term mental anguish. Once the shotgun was out of shells, pandemonium often broke out, so I quickly swapped for my rifle in case the animals decided to come in my direction rather than flee.

The big monsters would trumpet and crash away at full throttle. Dust and dirt filled the air, hanging like heavy clouds. Locals would watch the non-consumptive hunt from a safe distance as they shouted mightily at the departing elephants. The villagers would laugh and clap and enjoy the excitement. As I did.

A few minutes later, after tranquility returned, it was time to follow up on the crop-raiders. Often, the elephants determined that they'd run far enough and would stop short of their daytime loafing area. They'd linger and begin to feed on tree bark and bush, wait a short while, and then head back for another go at the maize field. I would fire more bird shot, zinging them again and again until they crossed back to the designated boundary. Most of the time it took multiple harassing melees to persuade the elephants to vacate back to their sanctuaries. Once my task was done and the crops were temporarily spared, I'd return to my Toyota and head back to camp.

I vividly remember after long chases through the fields and bush that I'd look like I survived a leopard mauling. Lacerations crisscrossed my body from my ankles to the bottom edge of my shorts, my forearms would be streaked in blood, and my face was always good for a slice or two. The thorny African bush is hard to navigate in low light while trying to keep up with an ambling elephant.

And There Were Elephants

When the tribal council decided a marauding elephant needed to be shot as compensation to the local people for damages done, the shotguns were left behind and replaced with big bore rifles. Rather than ambushing an elephant late in the afternoon, we would start tracking a bull at first light and stay on its tracks until we found it. Once the natives heard the final shot, they would descend upon us through the grass and trees.

Sometimes, a couple hundred men, women, and children arrived, carrying meat baskets and galvanized pails and plastic washbasins. They'd set to work on the animal with the goal of returning to their homes and villages with rations of protein to be sliced thin, sun-dried, and preserved.

The skinning of an elephant is part festive gathering and part angry riot. While skinners are busy at work, the spectating mob talks, sings, chants, laughs, argues, and shouts continuously. Once the skin, skull, and ivory are removed, the elders begin to butcher the meat. It wasn't uncommon for them to accidently chop each other with wild swings of axes and machetes. I've seen a man lose three toes, and concussions were common.

Once the meat is cut from bones and ready to be distributed, two lines form: one for men and the other for women. Village elders and safari staff oversee the raw meat portions handed out. The trunk is considered a delicacy and is given to the local chief. The safari company takes the skin, skull, ivory, and a small amount of meat. The natives take the rest. When everyone is gone, all that remains of the elephant is drying blood and the partially digested matter removed from the stomach. That's it. I can attest that more goes unused with a harvested whitetail deer than with an African elephant. No lie, no exaggeration.

April 24, 1997

Davison and I went to the Gorge area. I immediately bumped into a herd of cows and 1 young bull. We stalked to within 40 yards of them only to find no large bulls.

Several minutes later, we heard movement of more elephants a few hundred yards away. We stalked up to them in some very thick jesse. A very large anthill lay between us and the elephants. We climbed up the heap and immediately saw about 15 elephants directly beneath us. They surrounded the anthill.....It was the most incredible elephant experience I've ever witnessed. Only wish I had a camera...

A Spanish client was in camp and was hunting elephant. He wanted a bull with better-than-average ivory. Late one afternoon, I decided to explore a remote area, typically void of game other than the odd kudu bull and occasionally, elephants. I hoped to find a big bull with long tusks for the client. Davison, a young Tonga, and I quickly found a herd of elephants, but without any mature bulls. We soon heard elephants moving and feeding, and we moved in to have a closer look. A very large termite mound was directly between the feeding herd and us. We climbed it. Once I approached the peak, I realized the elephants were MUCH closer than I thought. The herd immediately surrounded the mound—they were only a few feet away.

Standing on the mound surrounded by elephants at very close quarters was, at first, deeply unsettling. Davison was a new hire, young, and inexperienced with elephant. When he saw the herd, he feared for his life, and in near panic, climbed the tree that protruded from the top of the mound. His eyes bugged out and resembled ping pong balls. I shouldered my .500 and I pointed the rifle at every elephant within ten feet of my position while I tried to keep my footing on the steep dirt peak.

I quickly saw there wasn't need to fear the herd. The elephants were oblivious to our presence. I gazed up at Davison, who climbed as high as possible and looked like he was perched to the top of a flagpole. I gestured that all was fine and he should climb down. I lowered my rifle and held it in one hand and hung onto the tree with my other. I relaxed, regained a regular breathing pattern, and watched the spectacle. Davison slowly and quietly climbed down the tree and stood next to me.

How the elephants didn't smell us is a mystery. A feeding herd surrounded us for twenty minutes or more. If I'd simply taken two steps down the mound with rifle extended, I could have touched several elephants on the tops of their heads. Their trunks reached up towards us, wrapped around branches and tree trunks, and stripped leaves and bark. I watched a cow nurse her calf only a few paces away. It was surreal.

My growing concern was that daylight was running out. The sun was setting fast and we were a considerable distance from the

Toyota. To frighten the elephant off from such close proximity could be dangerous, and besides, I didn't want to disrupt the family unit, which included several young calves. Eventually, the elephants moved off and it was safe to get off the mound. We scurried down the anthill, made a large loop around the herd, and jogged back to the truck. We arrived with only a few minutes to spare before total darkness.

The encounter was a "once in a lifetime" experience. Once I was back at camp, I told the story at the campfire.

To proclaim reverence for the wild animals I hunt and kill, to the non-hunter, might appear completely irrational. I grew up as a hunter and I struggle to explain the: "I love them and I kill them" paradox. For me, to hunt is a deep rooted freedom, stemming from my departure into a natural world of wild things and places. To kill is to have hunted, and I want to kill swiftly. I find no joy in death… only acceptance and understanding.

The late Finn Aagaard was a former Kenya professional hunter; and a highly-respected gun and outdoor writer. After Kenya's hunting ban in 1977, Finn and his wife, Berit, moved to the Texas Hill Country and lived on an acreage a short distance from the town of Llano. Finn was my mentor and I remember the day I first met him. On that first visit and after dinner, Finn signed my copy of his book, Aagaard's Africa. The inscription reads: "To Gordon White, a fellow African hunter, who has been there and seen the elephant, and loves it."

And There Were Elephants

Finn was correct. I do love the elephant and elephant hunting for many reasons. It's their size and power, their social structure and behavior, the giant bulls and little calves, and the long ivory (even if one side is broken). Elephant hunting has unequalled lore and history. It has famous hunters like Walter Bell, John Hunter, and Harry Manners. It's the classic British double rifles and their express cartridges. It's the long days of tracking, the endless miles, the heat and fatigue, the bluff charges and the real ones. It's finding the big tusker and getting real, real close. It's raising the rifle and the determined "moment of truth." And it's the immensity of the endeavor, the elation, and the reflective remorse. To hunt elephant is a pinnacle experience.

I'm fortunate to have spent time living in elephant country. Flipping through my journals, it reads as if I was among elephants every day. I think I was. I once saw a herd of elephants in the shadows of Mt. Kilimanjaro; they lumbered in single file, in a straight line that seemed a mile long. I've never seen so many pachyderms at one time. It was spectacular.

The day I killed my first elephant, I knew something changed in me. Was it an elephant hunter's the rite of passage? Maybe.

I shot more elephants after that first cow, including some old bulls with good ivory. The probability that I hunt another elephant is very small. But I'd like to think one day I just might find a solitary track—a huge one—and follow it long enough to see the magnificent beast that made it.

Yukon Days

September 13, 1993

I have a new hunter—Armin Penzinger from Austria. I called in a good bull 55"- 60." He crossed the river in the bend (3rd lookout) and walked towards us in the timber. Never saw him again. Driving home (8:30pm) we saw a bull in the water...

"No, no, don't shoot!" I shouted as I frantically waved my arms and shook my head. I was at the helm of my 16' aluminum skiff and I nearly plowed the boat into a full-size bull moose. Armin, my hunting client, was sitting at the bow as we rounded a sharp bend in the narrow, fast-flowing Nisling River.

The Nisling River flows in the southwestern area of the Yukon Territory. The river is crystal clear as it snakes through the Nisling range, across swampy flats, and then flows into the silt of the Donjek

River. The Donjek's grey water runs into the White River, and then finally spills into the mighty Yukon.

We'd been hunting moose all day. We'd stalked a big bull earlier in the day, but lost him in heavy timber. At day's end, while cruising back to camp, we had a trophy bull a few feet from the nose of the boat. My European sport, with rifle ready, wanted to shoot the moose while the animal was up to his neck in water, frantically dog paddling, and trying to get out of the water and onto dry land. My mind raced. A deep water kill brings ethical, moral, and legal issues, not to mention a serious meat recovery dilemma—a guide's nightmare. "Don't shoot!" I pleaded.

After skirting the moose, I slowly cruised downstream, all the while, looking over my shoulder. I watched the bull trot out of the shallows and onto the gravel bar. Water dripped off his dark hide. His height was shocking. I soon beached the skiff and led Armin through the willows. Camouflaged, I began guttural calls that imitate a cow in estrus. I quickly found the bull's tracks in the sand—we followed them as I kept calling. A short distance later, there he stood. Armin fired several shots from his 8×68s Steyr Mannlicher rifle and downed the bull near the bank of an oxbow.

This Yukon bull would not be the widest I'd ever guide, but he was my first. Armin didn't know this was a milestone for me, and I wasn't about to let him know. I kept the prideful moment to myself. The bull was a very good trophy with antlers that measured just a little under 60 inches wide. As we stood over the moose, I was mesmerized by the animal's girth—he was far bigger than I'd expected.

I turned to Armin to congratulate him and saw that he was clutching his chest. I don't speak German and his English was weak, but I deducted pretty quickly that he had heart health issues. The excitement of the hunt pushed his pulse to a dangerous rate and caused chest pains. Thankfully, after a few moments, he seemed to feel better. I was grateful that Armin didn't have a heart attack, or worse, die, but we still had a mature bull—dead—and only several precious minutes of twilight left to get downriver to camp. I had to move quickly. It's impossible to take a jet boat safely down a twisting river in the dark with logjams and boulders to navigate around.

I quickly dug into my daypack, pulled out my knife, and sliced open the bull's body cavity. I still remember how the entrails warmed my cold hands as I yanked them onto the sand and moss. This action allowed the body temperature to drop, thus, cooling the meat. It's unlawful to waste any game meat. It must be recovered and used for human consumption. I couldn't let the meat rot.

Before leaving the deceased bull, I laid a tattered sweater over withers, which is a trick to prevent grizzlies, wolves, wolverines, and scavenging birds from devouring the meat. Human urine is another deterrent, so I emptied my bladder close to the bull. Since Armin hardly knew English, I gestured with my hands for Armin to do the same. We made it to camp with a minute or two to spare, just shy of complete darkness.

Yukon Days

I don't recall how old I was—no more than 12 or 13, but I do remember pecking out a letter on my mother's electric typewriter, which was addressed to the Yukon Outfitters Association. I informed the association that I was interested in booking a Yukon hunt, which was not exactly a lie. I requested they send me brochures from the various outfitters who provided hunts throughout the majestic Canadian territory.

Whoever received and read the letter must have thought I was a potential client. The brochures arrived a few weeks later. Mission accomplished. I wanted the brochures for the black and white photographs of the noble trophies: full-curled Dall sheep rams, goliath moose, ferocious grizzlies, and the majestic caribou. I kept the brochures stashed in a manila folder in my parents' filing cabinet.

Years later, while in my parents' home in Montréal, I received a phone call from Ross Elliott, a Yukon outfitter. He asked me if I still wanted a job in the Yukon, and if I wanted to sign on with his outfit. If I took the job, I'd start by wrangling horses and getting camps ready prior to the hunting season, then, eventually I'd guide hunts. I told him, "Yes." After discussing arrival dates, other job responsibilities, and wages, I hung up the phone. I was going to the Yukon.

The Yukon Territory is the westernmost and smallest of Canada's three federal territories. It's bordered by Alaska, Northwest Territories, British Columbia, and the Beaufort Sea. Most of the territory is subarctic and is known for its long brutally cold winters and short pleasant summers. With these extreme northern latitudes, the daylight is brief in the winter months and lengthy in the summer. The total landmass is approximately 190,000 square miles and is made up of mountain ranges, lakes and rivers, black and white spruce forests, and tundra.

Long before the Europeans arrived to the Yukon, the territory was populated by the indigenous, First Nations people of Canada. The fur trade brought the Europeans to the Yukon in the nineteenth century. Missionaries soon followed. The Klondike Gold Rush of 1897 brought a wave of Europeans and settlements to this remote wilderness. Today, the current population is approximately 34,000 people with 90% living in Whitehorse, the territory's capital city.

I first arrived to the Yukon on July 1, 1993. My first month of work was spent gathering horses, which, at the end of the previous hunting season, were turned out into the wild hunting concession with no fenced pastures or stables, just mountains, forests, swamps, rivers, lakes, grizzly bears, and wolves, and a brutal cold winter to survive. The horses had to fend for themselves, a perilous existence. In early July, the bands of horses had to be found, chased down, rounded up, trailed to camp, shoed, and readied for the upcoming sheep hunts that began on the first of August.

The equine search commonly began from the air. Ross piloted the Piper Super Cub while I peered out the side windows and searched for herds of horses in valleys, creek bottoms, among the trees, and along grass-covered side hills. I knew little about these splendid animals, which didn't keep me from chasing herds of mustangs (on the verge of reverting to wild) at full gallop through heavy timber. During my pursuits, I fell off, got knocked off, and bucked off many a horse. I rode bareback, and crossed rivers and streams. I was kicked and bit. Although I never became an accomplished horseman, I became competent enough to ride and lead a pack-string through mountain terrain. On clear days, high above timberline, I could see the Yukon's Mount Logan—Canada's highest peak at 19,551 feet.

September 19, 1994

Picked up Harmon Maxson of Maryland on the 16th. We came up to the upper camp immediately after the hunt change on the Donjek. We were sitting and talking outside the hunter cabin in the early evening when we heard two moose fighting behind camp. I grabbed my binos and Harmon grabbed his rifle and we set off after the moose....

The nature of big-game hunting in northern Canada can be defined as difficult and challenging when things are going well. When things aren't going well, a successful hunt is almost impossible. Visiting sportsmen and their guides are, at times, dealt a heavy blow as they are challenged by rain, sleet, snow, brutal cold, relentless wind, low game densities, high mountain climbs, lost horses, broken boats, broken guns, and, sometimes, broken bones. Things go from bad to worse when you return to camp and discover that a grizzly tore the tent to tatters or broke into the cabin, ate the food supply, and destroyed everything else.

Harmon Maxsom's hunt was neither difficult nor challenging; rather, it was a gift. Harmon, a judge from Maryland, traveled to the Yukon with the intention of taking a trophy moose. By the time we got to camp on his first day, it was late, with no time to hunt. We were sitting on the narrow porch of the plywood cabin, discussing the hunt and getting to know each other when, suddenly, we heard clashing.

"What was that?" Harmon asked.

It wasn't a man-made noise. The next closest hunting camp was many miles downstream. More clashing. The sound was two bull moose fighting.

I told Harmon to quickly grab his rifle and ammunition. I fetched my binoculars. We started to jog towards the ruckus that was so close to camp. It was easy to stay on course towards the bulls as the fight grew more intense. There was no pause in the intense jarring of their antlers.

We moved from the open gravel bars into a dry muskeg of sparsely stunted spruce trees and scattered willows. I guessed the moose were no farther than a couple hundred yards away. The going was easy, the moss-covered bog was soft and quiet, and the visibility was perfect for approach. The fight continued and the hammering of the dry bone antlers grew louder and louder. I started to hear their heavy grunts, I saw thin trees topple and sway in the distance, but I still couldn't locate the bulls.

I asked Harmon to load his .270 Browning, ensure it was on safe, and to have the scope magnification turned down to 4X or 6X. We moved slowly, cautiously, and as we got closer, a gentle breeze drifted towards us—the wind was good. I stopped after every few steps, raised my binoculars, peered through the thin spruce, and searched for the two bulls. Nothing. The sun was setting, the light was gray and flat, and the air was cool. Everything felt right.

Through my binoculars, at about 100 yards, big brown shapes became visible; they were colliding and pushing one another. The grunts and clashing continued, skinny trees cracked and toppled. I saw that both bulls were mature. Their palms gleamed in the low light, but I had to get closer to study their antlers.

We moved in closer and closer. The big bulls didn't have a clue they were being stalked and watched by a hunter and his guide. I stopped our approach. We were close enough.

We stalked to within 20 yards of two bulls fighting in some small spruce timber.

It was a demonstration of power and fury—two Alaskan Yukon bull moose that weighed roughly 1,500 pounds and stood seven feet at the shoulder, trying to punish each other with all their might and strength. I was awestruck. The raging battle intensified, vapor shot from their noses and mouths, their long pink tongues hung out down below their jaws. They relentlessly charged each other, their long legs dug into the soft ground as they pushed and tumbled so close to us.

"Which one should I shoot, which one?" Harmon spoke anxiously into my ear.

"I don't know, I don't know!" I quickly responded. And I didn't.

I started to sweat, my heart raced. I could not decide which of them was the bull for the first day of our hunt.

Suddenly, the bulls stopped trying to kill each other and stood there, motionless. Did they hear us? I wondered. I doubted it. Did they smell us? Maybe. It was possible that wind may have swirled, but at that moment, it didn't matter why they stopped fighting. They just stood still and tall with streams of frost shooting out from their gaping mouths. One bull stood broadside and the other posed, facing directly away from us.

"Which one, which one?" Harmon begged.

"I don't know," I blurted back.

Both were excellent bulls, but I needed to see them head-on. I couldn't judge them well enough to make the decision. It was the first day of the hunt and I didn't want to make a mistake. The rut was in full swing, bulls and cows were on the move, courting each other along the river and in the vast open muskegs. I knew we'd also see many trophy moose on the next nine days of hunting.

A moment later, they began to trot off in their characteristic long-legged gait. Harmon and I hurried in their same direction. As I jogged, I let out a couple of cow calls, and low and behold, the big monarchs stopped dead in their tracks. The closest bull was maybe 30 yards from us. It stood in a small clearing and glared straight at us with his head high, his bulbous nose raised and exhaling, his antlers in full view and display. The spread was very wide, he had great palms, lots of points—I realized this was an exceptional bull. I'd told Harry to shoot the moose the moment he had a broadside shoulder shot.

A few seconds later, the bull turned, Harmon fired twice quickly, both shots were well-placed, the bull staggered a few steps, and went down. The hunt was over. It all happened so fast. The massive Yukon bull—the largest deer species in the world—lay on his side atop grassy tussocks and moss.

Harmon was ecstatic with his bull, and so was I. I leaned down hard on the exposed palm, which pulled the opposite palm out of the soft earth to reveal his great antlers. He was very wide. I cut a sapling to the length that measured the broadest spread from opposing antler tips, then pulled out my knife and sliced the bull from sternum to privates, gutted him, and threw my jacket over his head and neck. We walked back to the cabin.

After dinner, I privately measured the sapling I'd cut in the field. It stretched the tape to 69½ inches. Harmon's bull is the widest bull I've ever guided. The bull's antlers didn't surpass the glorified 70" mark, but that didn't matter. As they say in Texas, "He was plenty big."

The following day was spent packing out Harmon's trophy bull. I remember that it was a cloudless day, the sun shined, it was warmer than normal, and the black flies were horrific—a scourge drawn to the bull's dried blood on my hands, arms, and eventually, my neck and face. Those damn flies drove me crazy! For me, it takes seven arduous trips to move an entire boned-out moose with cape and antlers. By late afternoon, the backbreaking work was over, the fresh meat was wrapped in cheesecloth and hung from spruce poles in the shade a short distance from camp. A couple of hours of daylight remained, I went to work fleshing the oversized head skin. For the remainder of his trip, Harmon spent several hours each day standing and walking along the gravel bar, casting small spinner baits and spoons to grayling that seek the shallow riffles and deep holes along the banks of the river. The Arctic grayling is part of the salmon family, and is widespread throughout Western Canada and Alaska. The silver-colored fish has a large dorsal and is easy to fool, so catching several for dinner is a simple task.

Harmon had a wolf tag too, so for the next few days I routinely checked the moose's remains for signs of predators. Wolves never appeared, but one cloudless morning, I approached the kill site, and from a close distance (too close) a large grizzly rose from behind the mound of discarded guts, bones, and hide. I immediately dropped down and watched the bear. The grizzly was dark with a blocky head, a pronounced hump, and muscular shoulders and legs. The bear appeared to be a mature boar. After a few minutes, the bear disappeared behind the kill, which actually turned into a large mound of moss, grass, and everything else the bear could toss upon the remains. Grizzlies often cover their kills and discovered carcasses to mask the odor that might draw other scavengers. I went back to camp. Harmon was on the bank of the Nisling, and again, fishing for dinner. I told him a big griz was on his kill, but no wolves or sign of any.

The final days of Harmon's Yukon trip were spent relaxing in camp. We ate plenty of fish, delicious moose venison, read books, and slept in. On a few occasions, we cruised up and down the river in the jet boat and spotted moose—cows and calves, young bulls and some old ones. We never saw a bull bigger than the one we took on Day One.

On the last day of Harmon's hunt, I took him downriver to the Donjek, loaded his gear and rifle into the Cessna 185 float plane, helped the pilot strap his massive trophy antlers to the plane's struts, and bid him safe travels back to Maryland. I climbed back into my boat and motored upstream to camp. My next hunting client would arrive a few days later.

At the end of the hunting season, I was awarded a rifle for guiding the largest moose (Harmon's bull) among the outfit's guides for that season. The rifle, a Ruger in a .375 wildcat cartridge, has taken elephants, buffalo, leopards, one grizzly bear, several black bear, and an assortment of other game. I still own that rifle to this day. It stands in my gun safe and hasn't been fired in many years.

Most hunts are not as simple as Harmon's. To witness two giant bull moose—the kings of the far north—fight at close quarters is a thrilling and lasting experience.

I believe that wild sheep live in the most awe-inspiring country in the world. There is so much beauty in the home ranges of Canada's mountain sheep: the dramatic peaks and valleys, the lime-colored tundra slopes, the emerald alpine lakes, and clear mountain streams. In these mountains, wildlife is abundant in places and can be spotted from great distances. As well as sheep—caribou, grizzlies, and wolves roam this wondrous high country. The tectonic activity over millions of years has produced striking landscape. Sheep country is a paradise when the weather is good, but when a low-pressure system moves in and the weather turns for the worse—its sheer agony.

Late July 1996 found me in the Mackenzie Mountains in the Yukon Territory on route to spend a month hunting Dall sheep. I'd been back only a week from a six-month stint in Zimbabwe, where it never rained a single day for the entire safari season. Now I was close to the Arctic Circle, carrying living quarters and food for two on my back, and it rained every day from the moment I arrived in this mountain wilderness.

August 1, 1996
8:25 P.M.

All five of us are sitting at about 6,500 feet looking down on 8 rams, 25 ewes and lambs. From this high ridge we have also seen 5 caribou bulls, 2 of which are shooters. One of the rams is heavy and broomed – we hope Cheryl will kill him. He is about 1,000 yards below us – we plan to wait possibly till morning to make an approach. It has begun to be quite cold – this is why my handwriting is so untidy – cold hands! We will lay in our sleeping bags on the shale ridge.

About an hour or so after I wrote the above journal entry, thick low clouds approached quickly down the valleys and across the mountain peaks. The sight caught us by surprise. We were five in total: three guides and two hunting clients. Our sheep hunters, George and Cheryl Snyder from Maryland, were very experienced and passionate mountain hunters who were familiar to adverse conditions. My fellow guides, Mike Oleshak and Gord Wagner, were experienced, and we were all accustomed to miserable weather—it was nothing we hadn't seen before.

Yukon Days

The incoming weather system was a cause for concern. We quickly realized that we didn't have much time or any place to find shelter from the incoming system. We were positioned on a ridge, really a cliff, at 6,500 feet with the edge a few feet away that dropped straight down into a gaping abyss. Opposite the cliff's edge, a semi-steep grassy knoll sloped steadily down to the base of the mountain. We couldn't go anywhere. The situation became daunting. I was worried. We quickly took our tents from our backpacks and set them up in record time, threw our sleeping bags and a few essentials inside our dome quarters, and climbed in—George and Cheryl in one tent and three guides in the other.

The wind soon started to howl, and the rain began to pelt the thin fabric of our small tent. We were socked in and going nowhere. We just had to wait out the weather. Throughout the night, I remember the rain poured down harder and the wind grew stronger with lashing gusts that bent the tent poles, so much so that I thought they'd snap at any moment. If the gales had broken the tent poles, we would have ended up in a serious, possibly life-threatening, predicament. Water breached the tent and ran down the inside of the nylon walls. It soaked our sleeping bags, and everything that lay on the floor of the tent. I pulled my Leatherman from its sheath strapped on my belt, and used the knife blade to cut drain holes in the floor of the tent. It worked, the water drained, but we were wet and I was cold. The beautiful weather and living conditions of the African safari life were still so fresh in my mind. I thought as I lay there: *What the heck am I doing here?*

The following morning, the rain eased, but still fell from the dark clouds above. George and Cheryl were doing fine and had a positive attitude amid the extreme adversity. We needed to cook, eat, and drink some water. I grabbed a few water bottles and put them in my daypack. I set off down the slope to a small spring several hundred yards below our camp, which trickled out of the mountain and coursed down a shallow draw. The journey down to the spring and back up to the tent was treacherous. I remember the soaking wet grass and moss covered rocks. Thankfully, my hiking pole kept me from sliding down the slippery slope. We cooked food and heated water on a small MSR stove, ate MRE (Meals-Ready-to Eat), and drank hot chocolate, coffee, and juice made from flavored crystals. We were surviving and doing fine, but the weather had to break and clear at some point, which I hoped would be sooner than later.

Several times a day, the rain would cease momentarily and we'd leave our cramped tents and glass the higher slopes and lower valleys. We always spotted bunches of sheep bedded in protective cover that shielded them from the driving rain and wind. Wild sheep are used to enduring harsh weather.

In the late evening of our second night trapped on the ridge, while in our tent, Mike and Gord, and I thought we heard a faint droning sound. In the far north-eastern corner of the Yukon and atop a mountain peak, the only sounds naturally heard are: the howl of a wolf, the tumbling of a loose boulder down to chute, thunder, and wind. Not much else.

We looked at one another with inquisitive frowns that asked: You hear that? What is it? Moments later, we recognized the familiar chopping sound of helicopter rotors in the distance. The raw weather continued and we reasoned that the chopper was flying in for a rescue. Why else would a helicopter being flying in such awful weather? I wondered. The helicopter couldn't be coming for us as nobody knew where we were. We were totally off-the-grid.

The thud—thud—thud gradually got louder, and then eventually faded away. The night was quiet again with the exception of the random raindrops that struck the tent, and the occasional blast of wind.

We later learned that while climbing a mountain with a guide and client, a packer suffered a testicular torsion, or, as a wrangler told me, "The kid twisted his balls while he was hiking." I'm told this condition is excruciating and debilitating, and from a male's perspective, the ailment's definition is unnerving and horrifying. The packer stayed on the mountain (I assume in his sleeping bag and in a tent, but I don't recall the exact details) while the guide and client hiked back down the mountain and marched to a temporary camp that had a string of horses. The guide then traveled on horseback for eight plus hours to the main base camp, and finally, radioed for an emergency rescue. In those days, the Arctic Circle didn't have cellphone coverage and I don't remember ever seeing a satellite phone.

The young man with the unimaginable testicle condition stayed on the mountain, alone, for over 20 hours. When the helicopter finally reached him, they took him to Whitehorse for the medical care he so desperately needed. While the packer laid in a rocky crevasse on the side of the mountain in unyielding agony, I was in my camp feeling wet and cold. When I learned of his predicament I also realized I was lucky that my discomfort wasn't worse.

The minutes and hours ticked away on the ridge. The boredom was unavoidable and overwhelming. I fantasized about having a book to read. Backpack sheep hunts demand essential gear only and a book would occupy too much precious backpack space, which meant an entertaining novel was out of the question. I even left my journal behind and opted to bring several sheets of loose leaf paper to write my field notes, again, to preserve room for the necessary supplies.

The rain failed to stop and the temperatures continued to plummet. Hard winds came and went and soon the rain turned into snow, and, to our disgust, we woke up on the third morning to several inches of the white stuff. Life was getting tougher by the day. Jaunts down the mountain to fetch water were impossible, any attempt would be dangerous and likely cause a downhill slide for thousands of feet. We began to melt snow for cooking and drinking. Believe me, it takes a lot of snow to make five cups of steaming coffee.

August 5, 1996
9:00 P.M.

We have been trapped on the same ridge since August 1. That evening (Aug 1) it started to cloud over. We had to make camp on this high ridge..... We spotted the big broomed ram and his partner on the opposite ridge. Hopefully the weather will allow us to reach them tomorrow..... These four days have been absolutely miserable...... Very difficult conditions. George and Cheryl are very strong and kind people.

The morning of August fifth was the day we had been waiting for: the clouds disappeared, the sun came out, and it warmed up enough to melt much of the snow. We scouted some nearby passes in hopes of finding a safe route to take us off the ridge, bring us down below the snow line, locate a source of water, and start hunting sheep. We found a path and then packed up camp, including all our wet gear, and began our descent.

I vividly remember traversing a steep shale slope. Taking short steps, I placed one foot cautiously in front of the other along a skinny sheep trail as I carried my heavy backpack. I forced myself not to look right and over my shoulder and down to the valley floor thousands of feet below. The hundred yard stroll along the slender game trail was dizzying. I crossed the shale slope and, thankfully kept from tumbling to my death. We continued down through a rocky crevasse and ended up on a bright green snowless flat alpine bench with a sparkling cool stream, gorgeous scenery, and bands of sheep in several directions. It was Shangri-La. Life was good again.

The following days were actually pleasant. The temperature warmed, the sun shined more than it didn't, and the relentless winds became a comfortable breeze.

George shot his ram first: a beautiful animal with a full-curl and flaring horn tips. A really nice Dall sheep that Gord found close-by and actually first spotted through the tent flap while still in his sleeping bag. The following day was Cheryl's. We hiked and climbed into rugged habitat, endured one extreme vertical climb, found many sheep, spotted a few trophy rams, but failed to connect. The journey back to our two-tent camp on the grassy slope was long and taxing, we were depleted. A sense of joy overcame me when I could see my bright red and blue tent in the distance, and I thought, *Another 500 yards and we'll be home.*

Suddenly, a band of sheep came into view. The white sheep, 20 or so, were crossing the tundra bench between our tents and us. *How can this be? You've got to be kidding?* I thought. We dropped down and Mike and I pulled our spotting scopes from our packs. We studied the group of sheep and saw there was only one ram in the bunch; he was very old with massive broomed horns. He was close to full curl, but he certainly had more than the minimum of eight growth rings required by territorial game laws if a ram's horns fall short of full curl. Mike and I determined he was a legal ram and a worthy trophy. Cheryl wanted him and we went after him.

We stayed concealed within the contours and folds of the slope and managed to stalk within 250 yards of the sheep. This was as close as we could get. *Now or nothing.* I placed my daypack in front of Cheryl for her to use as a gun rest. She steadied her rifle, found the ram in her scope, and pushed the safety forward. She was ready to make the shot. I studied the ram one final time and confirmed that he was a great animal. A moment later, Cheryl's rifle shot broke the silence and echoed all around us. The old ram was hit. She quickly chambered another round, and fired once more. Again, the rifle's report rebounded off the mountains.

Yukon Days

Clearly visible on his bleach-white hide, we could see the ram was fatally hit. The band of sheep began to run, the ram followed his harem, and the entire group disappeared into a shallow draw. The females and youngsters soon reappeared on a further slope, but the ram did not.

We stood up, gathered ourselves and our equipment, and walked to the spot where we last saw the old male. We crested the low ridge and peered into a coulee below—there in the rocks and moss lay Cheryl's animal. The old boy was thin and beyond the years of prime health, his horns carried huge mass with blunt and broomed tips. His growth rings told me he lived for 13 years in this rugged country.

The next few days were spent relaxing and recovering. We caped, fleshed, and salted the sheep hides—preserving them for full-body mounts. We ate delicious sheep venison until we could eat no more. On the last day of the hunt, we hiked down to the wide valley below, met up with other guides and hunting clients, and rode horses back to base camp. A day or two later, I climbed into a DeHavilland Beaver bush plane and flew towards Whitehorse. My next hunt was in British Columbia.

Today, this hinterland remains largely untouched, and its animals are born wild and free. As a kid, I dreamt about going to the Yukon and hunting the game that dwells in that remote back-country. I did it, and I loved it…most of the time. I met great guides and horsemen. I worked with them and I learned a lot from them. These mountain men were tough—a tougher bunch than any other I've known. The hunters who travel to the Yukon who chose to walk and ride in pursuit of sheep, bears, moose, and caribou, are men and women with passion and perseverance. They have the grit required, which this Canadian territory demands, and they earn every animal taken. My Yukon days in its unbroken wilderness were hard and easy, but most of all, they're unforgettable.

Authors note: I went back to the Yukon in September 2009 and shared camp with Mike Oleshak. He hadn't changed much since our days trapped on the ridge. He was still a tough mountain guide. Gord Wagner passed away in 2015. He was 42 years old.

Buffalo Behave Badly

It was a hot April afternoon in the Zambezi Valley of Zimbabwe. Two friends and I stood in a thicket close to the edge of a maize field. An old photo shows my olive hunting shirt stained with sweat, blood trickling down my leg, and a frown on my face. A young bull elephant with very small tusks lay dead at our feet. He should've still been alive. I recall feeling remorse, even with the intoxicating adrenalin rush coursing through my veins.

Why did this elephant charge us? I wondered. *Did we get too close to him? Was it his aggressive nature conditioned from years of dealing with farmers whose fields he had been raiding?* I will never know the mind of the elephant, but what I do know is that his intentions were fatalistic, meaning death was inevitable.

Volumes have been written and many campfire discussions have been debated regarding which African animal deserves the highest distinction for being most dangerous. John Hunter believed it was the leopard, but his is a minority position. The hippo has been documented for killing more humans than any other animal, but in my opinion, hippos do not harbor true game animal status. Much has been attributed to the elephant, primarily due to its enormous size. It is easy for sportsmen to imagine, in graphic detail, extreme mutilation caused by a six ton animal when a hunter is overtaken and trampled and perforated by a long ivory tusk or two. I'm told that an enraged elephant, at times, will crush their victims by kneeling on them. To be killed by an elephant is messy. Period.

Those who hunt dangerous game have opinions as to which creatures give them the most shakes and shivers—and over time adventures can turn into tall tales, lies, or exaggerations. However, the following account that occurred during the 1995 safari season is the God's honest truth. It involves two friends of mine and one very formidable adversary: the Cape buffalo. The buffalo has a long-standing reputation for being an ill-tempered bovine, possessing vengeful traits, and seems to desire pleasure in remodeling hunters' physical features. Below is a buffalo hunt I'll never forget.

ZIMBABWE

August 3, 1995

The day of the buffalo!

Currie came up with Dudley to shoot a buffalo. We went to the gorge and looked for the 3 bulls that frequented the area. After an hour, we spotted 2 bulls and got within 10-15 yards but the jesse was too thick to get a shot or make out horns. They spooked and ran off. We decided to leave them and carry on towards Galagashi...

An old bull came out of a thicket...

Buffalo Behave Badly

*He came towards me in full bloody charge...when I fired my
second shot he could not have been more than 4 or 5 feet from me...*

Currie Pendleton, a well-mannered nineteen year old from
North Carolina wanted to kill a buffalo. He had accumulated
considerable African hunting experiences, had taken a lot of plains
game antelope species, and become a leopard connoisseur. Still,
Currie had never killed a buffalo.

His chance finally came and plans were made:

We packed two days' worth of gear and provisions in our Toyota
Land Cruiser and commenced an enduring voyage. Ten minutes into
our travels—tragedy struck. Dogs are plentiful, (some may say overpopulated in the communal lands of Zimbabwe) but serve a useful
purpose by keeping unwelcome predators at bay from farmers'
chickens and yearling livestock. On the road ahead, we spotted a
splayed-thought-to-be-dead dog on the hardtop. Etiquette asks us
to avoid running the tires over the dead canine and align the front
tires on both sides of the carcass in an effort to prevent guts, blood,
and meat from decorating the quarter panels of a vehicle.

We took the measured approach, and to our amazement, the
doggie was apparently having a mid-day nap under the searing
African sun. Our canine friend realized the grave danger a little too
late, and received a truck front bumper in the head at 120 km/hr.—a
deadly result for oversleeping. Currie had killed a villager's pet. At
first, I did not know what to say, and then decided to say nothing
at all. For the next hour or two, I remember the drive was without
much conversation. The mood was somber.

It took us three hours of horrible driving to reach our destination: the Manyoni. Along the way, we came upon a herd of fifteen buffalo bulls. Brakes were slammed, binoculars grabbed, and the evaluation of horns began. The herd stood motionless in the shade under a canopy of mopane trees. Several bulls were tremendous—over forty inches in width. One notable hard-bossed bull was close to forty-four inches. Currie was excited, but the problem was that these animals were inside a non-hunting area. We were not allowed to fire a shot. They were safe and they seemed to know it.

We reached the Manyoni and watched three young bull elephants browse at the river's edge and drink in one of the few remaining pools. The shadows lengthened, the air was now cool, and camp was set under towering acacia trees. We placed folding chairs and cots around a mopane wood burning fire, and positioned the Land Cruiser close enough to prevent a wandering elephant from stepping on us while we slept.

Robert, our jovial Shona camp man, served a fine meal of eland steaks, squash, and rice. After a few beers, we went to bed. My journal reads that it got very cold, I covered up with a couple of heavy blankets, the stars were bright, and I could easily see the Southern Cross.

Sunrise is the chilliest part of the day. A combination of shivering and the need to relieve myself woke me; but what got me out of bed was Albert, our tracker. He'd blurted out that he had sighted some buffalo not far from our camp. Currie and I actually caught sight of these buffalo from our beds. There were three very old bulls with hairless grey hides. They casually moved down the center of the riverbed. Each of the three bulls carried horns that looked like German army-issue helmets. Perhaps two-hundred yards from these three buffalo was a herd of about twenty. The herd was made up of cows, calves, young bulls, and a very decent older bull. As with the day before, these buffalo stood just inside the non-hunting area and, as the sun came up, they traveled deeper into it.

After some tea and toast for breakfast, we broke camp and went scouting for any buffalo that may have drifted into the hunting area. After a thorough reconnaissance effort, it was obvious that we were not going to find any "eligible" buffalo. We packed the truck and headed back to main camp. I was now behind the wheel as Currie was still a little shaken from decapitating the dog the previous day.

The following morning, Dudley Rogers—my boss, friend and professional hunter—announced over breakfast that he wanted to find an old *dagga boy* for Currie. I knew the whereabouts of three buffalo bulls that frequented a particular waterhole close to camp. We decided to go look for the bulls.

It did not take long to find tracks. Soup-plate sized imprints in the sand told us we'd found our bulls. I regularly saw three bulls in this riverine area, but *spoor* indicated that there were only two. *Where was the third buffalo?* The hot sun smothered us and the balmy breeze shifted constantly. I knew it would be almost impossible to approach buffalo with a swirling wind. The sign was not fresh and it looked as though the bulls had only come to drink the previous night. The wind settled and ceased to swirl. We began follow the tracks through thorn scrub, up and down numerous rocky hills, and finally to the edge of some of the thickest and nastiest jesse bush imaginable. I was confident that the bulls would be snoozing peacefully within the confines of the shade of this horrible vegetation. Dudley carried a Manton .470 double rifle, Currie carried my custom .375, and I carried an 8mm camera to video Currie's buff hunt. We proceeded slowly, inch by inch, looking everywhere for anything.

After an eternity of "Elmer Fudd–style" stalking, sneaking, and crawling, we found the two bulls. We weren't more than forty feet from the buffalo and hadn't the first clue if we were looking at an ass or a face. This brush was THICK! Before horns could be judged or even seen clearly, I felt the breeze hit my back—not a good thing. The buffalo immediately got our scent and determined we weren't other friendly buffalo. They grunted and crashed off into thicker and nastier jesse. We aborted any follow up for fear of pushing them into a neighboring country. The hunt was over for the moment.

The Land Cruiser was close by (perhaps a quarter of a mile). We decided to walk to the truck, enjoy some tea and biscuits, and then decide on the next plan of attack. I swapped my video camera for my .458. I slipped a solid in the chamber, checked my safety, and continued to follow Dudley and Currie through the dense thorn bush.

When not active in the pursuit of game, but simply meandering through the African bush to get somewhere, I admire the scenery, try to identify flora and fauna, or daydream of past hunts and experiences. This particular day was no different.

My thoughts drifted randomly when I, third in line, stepped down into a dry riverbed; then all of a sudden, and without warning,

Buffalo Behave Badly

a nearby bush began to shake and grunt. A split second later, a buffalo bull was charging straight for Dudley only a few feet away. Unable to shoot, Dudley's only option to avoid being hammered by the buff was too dive out of the way—and he did so with the grace of an Olympian. Currie and I instinctively shot the enraged bull with baby-carrot sized solids, but to no apparent effect. Within a few seconds, I went from gazing amateur naturalist to an extremely focused self-preservationist. I remember vividly that the scene became chaotic: heavy dust hung in the air, dirt was flying, people were shouting, and the buffalo turned into a huge black monster, seemingly confused on which human to attempt to run over next.

He picked me.

I had often read that buffalo, when charging, hold their head high; this, I can assure you, is true—although not enough has been said about the menacing look in their eyes and their flailing hooves. Here he came with manic fury. Another shot came from Currie's .375—although it didn't seem to help the severity of my situation. I had to do something—and fast.

Back-stepping barely gave me time to chamber another round. The buffalo was closing in and began to lower his head and horns to clobber me. I stopped back-stepping, re-shouldered the .458, pointed the rifle at his forehead and squeezed the trigger.

At the shot—which was no more than four or five feet from my muzzle—I noticed I failed miserably to hit his brain and drop the bull in his tracks. I quickly turned my back to the bull and swerved aside, expecting to be run over at any instant. Fortunately, the bull swerved as well, but in the opposite direction. I somehow regained composure, chambered my last round, and managed to pour one more shot into the fleeing animal. At a distance of about twenty yards, the buffalo stopped. It seemed too sick to run any further and turned to face us. While I was busy fumbling .458 rounds from my cartridge belt, Dudley and Currie advanced towards it and delivered the final, "strokes of mercy," to the old warrior. I didn't fire another shot. The bull stumbled down to the dirt, rolled onto his side, and a few short moments later, his death bellow echoed throughout the valley.

It was at this point we realized we had survived what very few ever experience. Our trusted tracker, Albert, had actually lied down to die. Pension, our government game scout, disappeared only to show up in camp a few days later. Currie had held his ground, performed under extreme pressure, and remained surprisingly calm. Dudley had a badly torn ear. I stood slightly weakened at the knees, bewildered by the terrorizing event. I realized I'd also avoided an accidental bowel release into my short safari shorts. Something of a miracle!

The bull showed signs of age and hardship with battle scars found all over his huge body. His tenacity and a vindictive nature most likely manifested from years of fighting off hungry lions and menacing poachers. *But why did he charge?* I still wonder to this day. *Did we startle him at such close quarters, causing a reactionary charge?* I could guess reasons all day long, though, in reality, I'll never know for certain.

What the encounter taught me is that attempting to designate one animal as the most dangerous is insufficient. The degree of

Buffalo Behave Badly

danger is relative to the situation at any given moment—whether it is tracking a gut-shot lion in the thick cover or having a swim in a crocodile-infested river. Fear is the emotional response to danger. One believes the elephant is most dangerous, while another proclaims the leopard is the bigger threat—both views are purely subjective and situational. At the crux of hunting dangerous game lies fear—and fear is personal.

Grandpa

My grandfather, Joseph Henry White, was born in 1892 and lived for ninety-five years. I knew him as "Grandpa," and I only remember him as being old. He had pale blue eyes, a pronounced chin, and commendable amount of white hair. When I spoke to Grandpa…I had to shout at him. My grandfather was almost totally deaf, and as a boy, I was always frustrated whenever I tried to tell him something. His son, my dad, explained to me that that Grandpa's hearing wasn't because of his age; he'd had a hearing impairment his entire life. Being "hard of hearing," which is what they called it back then, kept him from joining the Canadian army and fighting in World War I.

Grandpa's brother, Harold, did go and fight the Germans on French soil. In 1918, he received a head wound while in battle and was sent home to Canada. King George of England wrote my Great Uncle Harold a letter thanking him for: "his faithful services and wishing early restoration to health." The framed letter hangs

Grandpa

on a wall in my home. Harold died in 1924 from the head injury's unrelenting complications. Grandpa and Harold were very close.

In 1826, my grandfather's great-grandparents, James and Bridget White, left Ireland and sailed to Canada. They settled in St. Catherine-de-la-Jacques Cartier, a small community north of the St. Lawrence River in the province of Quebec. Years later, Grandpa's father, Charles White, built a resort called "The Lakeview House" on Lake St. Joseph, what was referred to as: "The Lake."

My grandfather grew up at The Lake. He married my grandmother, Holly Weir, in 1922. We called her "Granny." I have an old shoebox of faded black and white photographs of life at The Lake. Most of the photos include water, shoreline trees, rustic cabins, and canoes. The men all wore trousers, collared shirts, and often sported neckties. The women's vestments were plain dresses and large over-embellished bonnets, similar to what you might see at the Kentucky Derby, complete with feathers and bows. There was a sense of modesty, reminiscent of the times: no flip-flops, bikinis, dark tans, or beer cans in these photos.

Grandpa raced canoes. My bookcases and fireplace mantel hold the ornate silver trophies of regattas my grandfather won in 1909, 1913, and 1914. One of the trophies holds tail feathers of wild pheasants I shot many years ago along small creeks that led to the Yellowstone River in eastern Montana. An old Brittany named Heidi, found, pointed, and retrieved those birds.

My grandfather was an exceptionally strong swimmer and I remember a story my father told about how my grandfather saved a life. My grandfather was crossing The Lake by canoe with his cousin and a friend one October day. They were returning back from their wilderness camp after a week of hunting. A storm moved across The Lake, bringing high wind and rain as they paddled across the long stretch of water. Whitecap waves built up on the surface of the water and capsized the canoe. The men wore no lifejackets and struggled to keep their heads above water. My grandfather grabbed the friend, the inferior swimmer of the three, and swam him to the nearby shore. Grandpa's cousin drowned that day.

As a young child I recall seeing Grandpa walk right into the frigid lake; he'd never showed any sign of acclimating discomfort as he plunged into the water. He would then swim out to a distance barely visible from shore. Powerboats, water skiers, and windsurfers cruised and recreated between him and me while I stood on the brown sandy beach. I don't think my grandfather cared about the water traffic because he was nearly deaf, and with aging eyes, I doubt he could see or hear the weekenders as they raced past him.

I have early memories of The Lake. The drive to my grandparent's cottage was four hours by car from our home, and we always arrived in the dark of night. My grandparents owned a two-story white home on a big lot along a busy country road. The

Grandpa

"cottage" was built in 1927 and it had a cast-iron wood stove in the kitchen and a large brick fireplace in the living room. Walls and ceilings were paneled with Douglas fir, and the floors were pine. There was a small room off the kitchen that had a twin bed and a bookcase. The small library held old titles that carried the musty odor of aging reads. The book covers were hard and the pages yellow. I don't remember any specific titles, but do recall sitting on the soft little bed, flipping through the pages, and sliding the novels back into place on the shelf. Grandpa always told me I could take a book back home with me.

The front door led to a covered porch that spanned the width of the house. Throughout the porch were iron and wooden chairs complimented with a small table that held evening cocktails and an ashtray. My mother served midday ham and cheese sandwiches on white bread to Mike and me. Granny routinely delivered some imaginative dessert. I recollect a chocolate-fudge-gelatin slop of various textures. The porch's floorboards creaked and were painted high-gloss battleship grey.

The big yard was bordered by a tall hedge, which blocked the view of passing cars. Waist-high green ferns wrapped the outer wood walls of the cottage. The yard was really too large to cut with a walk-behind lawnmower, but a simple mower was what my grandfather owned and used. Dad and Grandpa argued on the sprawling lawn as to whose turn it was to cut the grass and when. My grandfather was incessant about pushing the mower himself and shaved the grass so short it burned yellow from blazing summer sun and heat. Behind the house stood a forest of hardwood trees as tall as they could grow. Along the timber edge, Grandpa slashed yard-encroaching tall weeds and understory with a rusty long-handled scythe. The toolshed was a rough room that seeped traces of oil, wood, grease, and gasoline. Nails driven into the delaminating plywood walls held an array of adjustable tools. Wrenches, handsaws, screwdrivers, hammers, and crowbars lay strewn on the table. Old coffee cans held screws, washers, and nails. An old Johnson outboard motor stood on its skeg in a corner next to dark grey paddles whose lacquer had worn off many summers ago.

Our summer days at The Lake were spent swimming, canoeing, and fishing. After an early breakfast, we carried paddles, lifejackets, fishing rods, and heavy steel tackle boxes and walked the narrow path to the water's edge. Grandpa always had two canoes, and when they weren't in the water, they laid flipped and tipped against shoreline alders at lake's edge. They were too heavy for a young kid to overturn and push across the gritty sand into the shallows. At the beginning of each season, Grandpa swept a fresh coat of emerald green paint along the hull, from stern to bow, and covered the recently glued leakproofing fiberglass patches.

Mike and I paired with either Dad or Grandpa and we'd paddle from the bow and they stroked from the stern. I often pestered my father to buy a boat with a motor; the plodding pace by canoe was hard work for a kid. Canoe travel was too leisurely for my youthful impatience and my need for speed. We paddled to Blueberry Beach, a favorite spot to catch smallmouth bass. There was a sunken steamboat a short distance from the beach's shore, which provided great structure for fish and other aquatic life and vegetation. Behind

Grandpa

the beach was a backwater fringed with cattails and bulrushes. The canoes were portaged across the short stretch of sand, and then we slid them into the murky swamp. We slowly paddled into the brackish water and lowered a minnow trap into the water with hopes of catching the next day's bait. The following morning, we'd return to the backwater and retrieve the traps by towing in the float first, then we'd pull the length of yellow nylon rope hand-over-hand until the bait trap was out of the water and in the canoe. Without fail, the steel mesh net held abundant minnows. We went fishing. Mike and I used our trusted Zebco spin casters: white rods and black reels. Dad fished with his blue fiberglass rod and open-faced spinning reel; Grandpa held his bamboo fly rod, but without wet flies, and joined his progeny's uncivilized approach to angling with lively baitfish. Bass eat minnows.

I remember a morning as I watched my grandfather's vintage silk fly line suddenly cut through the water. I knew that he had a fish on the line. A big bass broke the surface of the water and was desperately attempting to cough out the minnow while airborne. Meanwhile, Grandpa was focused on lighting his pipe with his chrome Zippo lighter, which resulted in a progression of hair-singeing flames followed by billows of pungent smoke wafting above the canoe that enveloped me while I shouted, "Grandpa, you have a bass!"

He didn't hear me and lacked concern for his rod, which was flopping about his legs and rattling on the bottom of the boat. Eventually, he succeeding in lighting the tobacco and the big smallmouth continued to vault out of the water and dance like a tailing tarpon. It's a favorite memory of mine, which I remember like it was yesterday.

We always killed the fish we caught. "Catch and release" was a regionally unaccepted practice. The act of catching a fish only to unhook it and allow it another day in the water seemed foolish. As a kid, I remember spending long hours and many days sitting on a mesh seat in the bow of the canoe and reeling in smallmouth bass, but I don't recall ever eating one. Growing up in Quebec, we ate salmon and trout but never catfish or bass. Mike and I held the stringer or creel as high as we could reach for Mom and Granny, sitting above us on the cottage porch, to inspect the fish. They seemed impressed with our catch of smallmouths, but I suspect that Grandpa's cat, Poopsie, was more impressed and ate the mess of dead fish soon after we tossed them in the woods behind the cottage.

There were days we decided to fish for brook trout. The dainty dark green and red speckled "brookies" didn't measure more than six or eight inches and were caught in tiny creeks and streams accessed by long walks through vast boreal forests. On the dark nights prior to our trout trips, Dad, Mike, and I, with flashlights in hand, hunted for night crawlers on the cottage lawn. Once our quarry was spotted in the light beam, Mike or I pounced on the giant worm before it raced through the grass and into the soil. Night crawlers are fast, but the skinny kids snatching them were faster. The worms were kept in an old coffee can packed with moist soil and breathing holes were driven into the lid with nails. Of course, the night crawlers had to breathe and survive until the moment they

Grandpa

were threaded onto a treble fish hook. Worms wiggling with vigor were essential for our trout fishing forays.

The approach to brook trout catching is simple: lower hooked worm, secured to a short length of monofilament affixed to freshly cut tree limb into small freshwater stream; wait until little trout ingests worm and hook; then jerk the fish out of the cool clear water. We ate the delicious tender dainty trout. Poopsie the cat never ate one of our brookies—my mother saw to that.

I recall hunting with my grandfather only on one occasion, and the memory is a brief snapshot. Dad, Grandpa, Mike, and I walked down a trail, the sun shined and I remember tall hardwoods and spruce trees. My grandfather might have been ninety years old and walked slowly. I complained about his quiet pace and told my father that he should have stayed at the cottage. Reflectively, I feel a tinge of guilt for the selfish words and attitude, but I sense my grandfather didn't hear me moan my impatience. We didn't find any partridge that day.

The first deer I killed was a whitetail doe. She was a big doe and I shot her with an iron-sighted Winchester Model 94 .32 Winchester Special. I sat against a tall tree on a steep slope below a ridgeline close to the shore of a lake. I heard leaves crunching at intervals growing louder and louder until two deer came into view. I took the lead doe. The following Sunday, my family and I went to my grandparents' apartment in Montréal for an afternoon visit as we routinely did every Sunday after church. My grandfather sat in his big arm chair wearing oversized headphones with their coiling black wire plugged into the television across the room. My father leaned over and asked Grandpa to remove the headset. Dad then told him, "Gordon shot his first deer last weekend."

I stood next to my father and looked at my grandfather. Grandpa then looked back at me and asked, "Did you feel bad?"

I replied, "Yes."

He said, "Good," and slid the headphones over his ears and went back to watching the television. My grandfather was a true outdoorsman: a "coureur de bois," and spent much of his long life on the water and in the woods. He raced canoes, fished, and hunted. I believe my grandfather asked me the question to find out if I respected wild animals and wild places and that I didn't hunt for the sake of killing alone.

Today I have my grandfather's canoe racing trophies, a shoebox full of black and white photographs, his old burgundy sweater, several bamboo fly rods, reels, and a wallet of assorted wet flies. I wish I had one of his old pipes or even one of the heavy wooden green canoes; but I don't and that's okay. I haven't been back to The Lake, and the cottage was sold a long time ago.

The last time I fished with my grandfather, he was ninety-three-years old and he paddled the canoe with force from the stern. I can't remember how many smallmouths we got that day, but I'd

Grandpa

like to think the day was extraordinary because, the truth is, my
grandfather was just that: extraordinary.

Blitzing Bluefish and Martinis

MAINE

August 18, 1992

I guess the urge to catch bluefish was initiated by Ruark's Old Man and the Boy stories... Greg, Rick, and I made plans to go to Maine for a few days... We drank a few Old Brown Dogs... The fishing was fantastic. Rick caught eight on light tackle, Greg caught three, then broke his reel, and I caught six. We hooked and lost several others...

My longtime friend, Rick Cox, and I stepped out of a pub onto a dimly lit sidewalk on a narrow street in Portsmouth, New Hampshire. We then walked to a dark, unoccupied parking lot a couple of blocks away where we'd parked the car a few hours earlier. It was after midnight, and Greg Carson, another childhood buddy, planned to meet us at this lot sometime before dawn.

Blitzing Bluefish and Martinis

It was summertime. College classes would start soon, and I was about to begin my last semester before graduation. Greg's academic pursuits were also ending, and Rick was about to move to British Columbia to start graduate school. We agreed that we deserved a short recess from our menial summer jobs, and that we should hang out for a few days at the Maine Coast.

I never considered myself a "beach" person. I had no interest in sunbathing, and swimming in the ocean bored me. I found snorkeling for sand dollars momentarily entertaining. I tried boogie boarding—once, but got badly hurt while trying it. Jellyfish scared me. I agreed to this trip to the coast for two reasons: to hang out with my friends—and to catch a bluefish.

One of my favorite writers, Robert Ruark, wrote stories about fishing for bluefish with his grandfather in his "Old Man series." I'd never seen a bluefish, but I thought I needed to catch one. I read that they're voracious feeders and fight hard once hooked.

Bluefish are a popular game fish and are found off the coasts of South Africa, Australia, and Southeast Asia. They also live in the Mediterranean, Black Sea, and along the U.S. Eastern Seaboard as far north as Nova Scotia. These fish are aggressive and strong, live in loose groups, and are fast swimmers. When schooled, they ferociously feed on forage fish. The little sardine-like prey fish are pushed to the surface, and often into the surf zone, where they are attacked and devoured in very shallow water until all the baitfish are dead or the bluefish have filled their bellies. This frenzied feeding is sometimes called "the bluefish blitz."

Bluefish must be handled with caution; they have sharp teeth, commonly grow to 20 pounds, and have been reported to attack people while they are wading and swimming. I wanted to catch at least one.

In anticipation of our trip, I had spoken to Art, a salesman, in the fishing department at the famous outdoor outfitter, L.L. Bean, in Freeport, Maine. Art told me the bluefish were schooled up and blitzing up and down the nearby coastline. It was time to go fishing!

Based on my conversation with Art, the three of us had made a plan. So, once Rick and I reached the lot, we retrieved our camp cots from the car, unfolded them, laid down, and covered up with old wool military surplus blankets. We faded off to sleep with the occasional sound of a passing car or a honking horn in the background. We were cash poor and too broke to get a motel room, so naturally, sleeping in an empty parking lot seemed like a good idea.

At some point during the night, I woke up, my head and hair soaked from the early morning condensation, and realized that Greg had arrived. He'd parked one lot over and was sound asleep in a mortuary pose on a cot next to Rick and me. We were lucky that we had not been spotted by the local police passing by. At sunrise, we gathered our cots and dew-soaked blankets, and drove off to find a place for breakfast.

After we ate, we headed straight to the L.L. Bean to buy the appropriate fishing equipment. My experience was as a fly fisherman, so I had no spinning or surf casting gear. I learned that the farthest distance I could fly cast a big streamer would likely fall far short of feeding bluefish. I deferred to using a heavy surf

Blitzing Bluefish and Martinis

rod to cast a six-inch fluorescent top water plug with dangling treble hooks tied to a steel leader. The three of us bought low-end saltwater surf "packages," which included a rod, reel, and a spool of monofilament. We also purchased a dozen vicious saltwater lures and some steel leaders. Art told us the blues were actively feeding at York Beach.

We drove in tandem, Greg in one car and Rick and I in the other. We headed to York Beach, southward along state highways that follow the jagged, rocky coastline. As a kid, my family vacationed at Old Orchard Beach; we stopped there for a moment and looked around. Then we decided to check out Kennebunkport, a quaint coastal village first incorporated in 1663 that was quickly depopulated by Indian depredations. Years later, this idyllic town was resettled and became a shipbuilding center. It became best known as former President G.H.W. Bush's summer home. I have a photo of Greg and Rick at Walker's Point, arms around each other's shoulders. The backdrop is a gray sky heavy with clouds along the dark Atlantic Ocean. By late afternoon, we had arrived to an unremarkable campground at York Beach. We pitched our small dome tents, and placed our cots and bedding inside the simple living quarters. The beach was within walking distance from our campsite, and small seaside resorts buzzed with some human activity. We strolled down a quiet two-lane road that followed the contour of the rugged coastline and bordered the brown sands of the local beach. We found a seaside hotel with a promising restaurant and bar. From our dining table, we could see waves breaking on the beach and the last of the sunbathers and beachgoers packing up their chairs and towels as daylight seeped away. Our waitress told us the hotel was built in 1868 and its earliest guests arrived by horse-drawn carriages and steam train. Back then, I had scant appreciation for the old world charm or historical aspects of unique places such as the hotel. At that moment, I was only mindful of catching a bluefish and a good meal. We started with martinis—first as pre-dinner drinks, and then as dinner drinks, and I think as post-dinner drinks, too. We might have been without enough funds for a modest motel, but for some reason, we were financially flush for food and beverages.

After a gluttonous seafood dinner, we moseyed over to the bar and pool table, ordered pitchers of beer, played eight ball, and tried to make friends with the locals. Later in the night, our waitress cut us off, ending our evening at the historic coastal resort.

When I woke up the next morning and crawled from my tent, I noticed the sun angled down through the tall trees from high above. It was well past sunrise, and, I'm ashamed to say, our campsite looked like a homicide scene that should have been cordoned off with yellow police tape. Greg was asleep in the backseat of his car, back door ajar, legs stretched out. Rick was snoozing on the floor of his tent next to his cot, the flap unzipped, with his legs sprawled outside on the pine needles and dirt. It looked bad. There were adults and children in neighboring campsites; families trying to enjoy wholesome outdoor experiences, cooking on gas-burning stoves, throwing Frisbees and horseshoes and footballs, packing up for a day at the beach while three college-aged morons appeared unconscious and dispersed at their campsite. I shouted to the guys to wake up.

Blitzing Bluefish and Martinis

It had been a long hard night of overconsumption and nobody felt good. We carried our camp chairs to the beach and figured a short nap was needed before we attempted to do any fishing. The bright sun, cloudless sky, easy breeze, and gentle noise of breaking waves quickly put the three of us to sleep. After several hours, I stirred. I was rested and felt alive again, but my skin seemed a little tender. Greg and Rick were still knocked out and looked peaceful slumped in their beach chairs. Rick and I wore shorts and t-shirts, but Greg only wore shorts. We failed to apply any sunscreen prior to our seaside snooze. The guys looked like they'd been under a heat lamp and I'm sure I did too. It was too late to do anything about it now. I woke them. It was time to go fishing.

With the help of a favorable wind, I could cast the gnarly plugs almost out of sight. Cast after cast into the surf was fruitless. York Beach was a bust. We didn't catch any bluefish or any other fish for that matter. From a nearby pay phone, I decided to call Art. Our salesman now told me that the bluefish were seen in the mornings in big schools near a railroad trestle bridge in Casco Bay at the East End of Portland. We packed up our camp, convoyed to Portland, and easily found the trestle bridge.

It was early evening when we arrived at Casco Bay with an hour or so of daylight remaining. By now, collectively, our hangovers had dissipated nicely, but the effects of protectionless overexposure to a glaring sun became apparent. The skin on my lower legs, arms, and face was tight and extremely sensitive to the touch. Rick's symptoms mirrored mine, but Greg's were worse. His face and extremities were also cooked, but his chest was so severely burned that it glowed. It looked bizarre.

We forged ahead. The shorelines and trestle bridge were void of anglers; the place was desolate. We walked along the rocky shoreline, stepping around and over beer and soda cans, plastic and paper debris, an assortment of trash that washed up and occupied unkempt beaches. Also, there were fish carcasses everywhere in various stages of decomposition. These were the first bluefish I'd ever seen. Many of the maggot-covered dead fish were tenpounders or bigger, sunbaked, dry, brittle, rotting. Hacked heads with gills attached were scattered about, and fish skeletons and bones were strewn all over the rocks and sand. A million flies buzzed. The stench was overwhelming, causing minor, sporadic heaving and retching. As we stood under the tall trestle and looked at the rocky shoreline, it was plain to see that Art was correct—fisherman were catching and killing bluefish at this spot.

By late evening, our cars were parked at the end of the gravel path that ran parallel to the train track and stopped at the peak of a knoll that overlooked the shoreline and inlet. We decided to sleep in our cars. It was a brilliant idea, cost effective, and the simplest thing to do. We were tired and suffering terribly from sunburnt skin. At that time, and in our health condition, any attempt to erect our tents was totally out of the question.

Sleep was fitful. I was feverish and miserable. Greg and Rick were no different. We moaned and complained continuously through-out the night.

Blitzing Bluefish and Martinis

When the sun began to rise over the Atlantic, we slowly got out of our cars and compared our varying shades of red skin. Greg's chest was a concern with its leaking sun blisters and growing boils. We drove to town; scarfed down eggs, toast, and bacon, and then returned to our parking spot that overlooked the inlet. Soon men, women, and children began to arrive with long heavy rods, large spinning reels, tackle boxes, and five-gallon buckets. The space on the trestle bridge was filling up with fishermen and their families, shoulder-to-shoulder along its entire length and more were lining the water's edge. We unpacked our surf rods and walked down the grassy slope to the rocky shore. We waited.

Before long, hollering and shouting was heard from the high trestle. Churning water and swooping seagulls were spotted in the distance and approaching. We got ready.

And then it all happened at once. Heavy plugs were simultaneously cast from the trestle bridge and the shore fisherman nearby. Bluefish were in front of us, feeding ferociously, breaking the surface of the water, making it appear as if it were boiling. White gulls hovered and dipped cautiously to pick bits and pieces of the mutilated baitfish that floated in the melee. Greg, Rick, and I started casting our treble-hooked lures into the frenzied waters. It seemed as though everyone was hooking fish. Big bluefish were reeled upward 30 feet from the water surface to the top of the trestle bridge. I remember hooking my first bluefish, and at the time, it was the largest fish that I'd ever hooked. My big fiberglass surf rod arched over hard and the fish's fight put heavy strain on my shoulders and arms. Eventually, I reeled the fish in close, through the shallows, and onto the dark sand and stony beach. I grabbed the fish by his broad forked tail and held it up. The fish was big—likely a fifteen-pounder.

While still holding the fish by the tail, I laid him back down on the sand and noticed his row of sharp teeth; I then reached into my back pocket and retrieved my long needle-nose pliers and twisted the treble hook loose from inside the bluefish's jaw. As I was about to release the big fish back into the water, I heard a soft voice call out behind me. It was an elderly Asian man who stood a short distance away with his hands held behind his back. He approached me, and then gestured that he'd like to have the fish. I walked toward the man and carefully handed him my first bluefish.

The bluefish continued to "blitz" and I kept hooking fighting them until I was tired and worn down from it all. My buddies were busy catching big blues, too. Rick caught the most fish, and Greg snapped the handle off his reel while fighting a heavy one. We watched a huge sea lion engulf a large blue as a fisherman started to heave the fish above the surface of the water to his perch high overhead on the trestle bridge. The bluefish was eventually pulled out of the seal's mouth as the fisherman pulled back so hard on his rod that I thought it would snap at any second. I'd hoped the seal would've won that tug-of-war.

We were done. The blitz ended as abruptly as it started. The intense action of catching the bluefish momentarily numbed the pain of our sunburns, but once we were back in our cars and driving off, the severity of our carelessness came to light. My skin was on fire. Rick was hurting too, as he stared out the passenger

Blitzing Bluefish and Martinis

side window, silent, gazing at Maine's mountains and forests as we
sped towards the Canadian border. Greg drove home solo.

Today, I still don't care much for the beach, sunbathing,
jellyfish, or boogie boarding. My college days are thankfully over.
Today I'm a parent and, hopefully, make better decisions. Greg
and Rick are still great friends with families and careers of their
own. I don't think any of us have caught another bluefish since that
trip many years ago. I like to think that perhaps one day, I'll catch
another big blue—but next time, I want to land one with my fly rod.
And if I ever decide to visit Maine's coast again, I'll stay in a B&B,
motel, or hotel rather than my car; and, I'll load up on sunblock and
as for the martinis, well....

Mike (left) and I pose with ruffed grouse our dad shot on a Quebec "partridge" hunting trip. As kids, we anxiously waited for his arrival from hunts to see what lay in his game bag.

Dad holding a ruffed grouse on the banks of the Gatineau River in central Quebec. I recall that my father used a single-shot .410 for most of his ruffed grouse hunting.

My grandparent's summer home at Lake St. Joseph. The "cottage" was built in 1927 and it was at "The Lake" that I learned to swim, paddle a canoe, shoot, and fish.

My grandfather holds a smallmouth bass while standing near a remote wilderness cabin he built. Grandpa was an exceptional swimmer, paddler, and angler. He was at home both on the water and in the woods.

In 1992, childhood friends Greg Carson (left), Rick Cox (right), and I (be-low), on our summer break from college classes, traveled to the Maine Coast for bluefish. We caught some big blues on a "blitz."
It was a memorable low budget trip.

Professional hunter Mitch Bunce (right) and I pose with a crop-raider bull elephant. Starting at first light, we tracked the bull from a villager's field and caught up to him a few hours later along a dry river bed.

An Austrian baron (right) and I with a trophy Yukon moose. I called the bull in from across a large muskeg. Packing out the bull took an entire day, which was back-breaking work.

Mike (right) and I on a cold day in Saskatchewan. Hunting Canadian wilderness whitetails is difficult and the weather can be brutal.

Jim Moses (right) and I enjoyed great hunts for Alberta whitetails. Jim took this buck at last light on a frozen stubble field.

The buffalo that nearly got us! This bull was very old and ill-tempered. Currie Pendleton (right) stood his ground and kept shooting during the charge.

Mike (right) and I with a big leopard. Mike was in the blind when the client shot the cat. Notice the leopard is missing a hind foot likely lost to a poacher's snare when he was a younger cat. He was a big, healthy male that, obviously, caught his prey on three legs.

My brother Mike with the "Steffy" buck—one of the finest whitetails I've ever seen. A monster Alberta whitetail hunted in true fair-chase fashion.

British Columbia is a wildlife paradise with an abundance of grizzly bears. This big grizzly was taken late on the last day of the hunt.

Mike (right) and I with the Zimbabwe lion that killed donkeys and cattle. For more than a week, this lion and a lioness spent their days in an acacia thicket behind a tribal community school and hunted livestock at night.

The late Finn Aagaard (right) was a mentor and inspired me to explore and hunt Africa. While visiting Finn and his wife, Berit, at their home in the Texas Hill Country, I asked to see his rifles. I'm holding his trusty Winchester .375 that his clients and he used on safari in Kenya.

A buffalo cow I shot at the request of a tribal chief. In Zimbabwe, buffalo are often hunted in thick bush. This cow was shot at 11 paces.

Camden with his first whitetail buck. He's a great shot and he took this buck with one well-placed bullet.

Cade poses with a nice South Texas buck taken across a food plot. Like his brother, Cade is a fine shot with a rifle and shotgun.

Lamar Wakefield took this buck in an Alberta wheat field. When we reached the buck, I was shocked at the body size of this mule deer. He tipped the scales at 381 lbs.

Some of my most memorable days afield were spent guiding bobwhite quail hunts in South Texas. Son (left) and Jasper (right) were big running pointers that never quit hunting. These dogs were tough and pointed covey after covey.

In 2013, I hunted Yellow-necked spurfowl, sandgrouse, and guinea fowl in view of Mt. Kilimanjaro. Our Masai guides were excellent. Kenya closed bird hunting shortly after this hunt.

Baja Mexico is one of my favorite places to hunt. Next to me from left to right, David Higman, Dan Higman, and Greg Henicke pose with Gambel's quail after the last "drive" of the day. Driven quail are extremely fast targets.

Mearns quail hold well for pointing dogs and they live in beautiful country. Col. Dennis Behrens (right) and I at the end of a day's hunt in southern Arizona. The Colonel is one of the finest sportsmen I know and rarely misses a bird.

Hunting brown bears on the Alaskan Peninsula is a world-class experience.
Brad Brock's bear hunt ranks as one of the finest hunts I ever witnessed.
His bear squared 10'4"—a true monster.

Hunter Wood (left), Brian Huntley (center), Finley (front), and I take a break during a vintage South Georgia bobwhite quail hunt. Finley rode the wagon and horseback on a gentle Tennessee Walker. She also helped the Labrador Retriever find downed birds.

(Left to right) Tommy Dugger, Ricky Lester, and I pose with an Asiatic water buffalo taken in Arnhem Land in Australia's Northern Territory. This part of the world is extremely remote with high populations of buffalo, wild pigs, wild ox, dingos, and crocodiles. It might be the wildest place I've ever hunted.

Big Canadian Deer

The gray light was dwindling as snowflakes drifted down. I was perched uncomfortably on baseball-sized clods of snow-covered earth as the scent of stale dirt wafted in the cold breeze. I propped my elbows on my knees and glassed the big landscape all around me. Down the slope, and a couple hundred yards distant, a rusted five-strand barbed wire fence separated the farmer's fields and cattle pastures. Some livestock grazed and moved along the banks of a slithering, slow creek, which weaved through the white grassland dotted with willow thickets before disappearing into an immense spruce and poplar forest. The vision of ravens on the horizon was haunting.

It was the last day of the 1997 Alberta big game season. Since opening day, I'd been guiding clients, without a break, hunting for bear, elk, moose, and deer. This late afternoon hunt was for me, not for a client.

Big Canadian Deer

Deer were beginning to appear: does, fawns and a couple of young bucks carrying small racks. The whitetails ambled cautiously towards a favorite food source: alfalfa. During most daylight hours, the deer remained in the sanctuary of the big timber. As the sun began to set, they moved cautiously towards the lush alfalfa field that bordered the cattle pastures.

The drab sky was darkening. I searched every edge and nook with my binoculars. Suddenly, a dark-bodied buck appeared a few steps from a stand of short willows. Even from a great distance, he was a large deer. I saw ice caked on his swollen neck and along his swayed back. His nose looked stubby and his head looked like that of a bull. His belly sagged and his hocks were stained black all the way down to his hooves. His chocolate colored rack was slightly wider than his ears, grew tall tines, and carried thick mass to the end of his main beams, which is the signature characteristic of big Canadian whitetails. I noticed a few kickers and oddball junk too. This buck was a goliath and I wanted a shot at him. With ten minutes or less of shooting light remaining, I had to close the gap from where I sat on the high ridge.

I got up, slung my rifle over my shoulder, and jogged down the slope. I dropped from the buck's sight and moved in his direction. At the end of my sprint, I reached the fence line at the edge of the field. Several deer, does and fawns, moved to my left, but I didn't see the buck anywhere. With precious minutes of light left, I unzipped my heavy jacket and pulled out the grunt tube that hung from my neck. I blew into it a few times, hoping to draw in the big deer. My .300 Magnum sat propped on a rotting cedar fence post with my thumb gripping the safety. I blew into the tube again and two does came charging out of a low swale to investigate the "deer" grunting with vigor.

They stopped suddenly at twenty-five paces, spying not a deer, but a man wearing a camouflage jacket and black wool knit cap. The deer stomped their front hooves in disapproval and snorted blasts of frosted vapor into the air. Seconds later, a mature buck came into view slightly behind the does. I peered through my scope and found the big whitetail in my crosshairs. I pushed the safety forward. I looked the deer over and quickly realized he wasn't the bruiser I spotted from the crest of the hill. The buck was mature and in his prime, he carried a good rack with long tines. He was a good trophy, bigger than any buck I ever killed, but he wasn't the one I wanted.

I thumbed my safety back to the safe position, slung my rifle, stood up, and watched the deer prance off with their white tails standing high above their backs and switching left-right-left-right. Legal shooting light came to an end.

This deer season was over and I ambled back through the hard crusted stubble and shallow snow and reached my old Ford pickup in the dark night. I sat on the cold hard bench, shivering. I started the engine, cranked the heater to the max, and exhaled warm breath into the palms of my frozen hands. That was a good hunt, I thought.

Big Canadian Deer

My brother Mike and I read stories in North American Whitetail magazine of the huge bucks of western Canada. David Morris, Dick Idol, and Russell Thornberry were my whitetail deer mentors and wrote fascinating stories of three hundred pound plus behemoths with record book racks. These great bucks became nocturnal ghosts, impossible to outsmart, and impossible to kill. Their hunting tales of the brutally cold Canadian north woods and desolate farmlands filled me with an unbounded sense of adventure in the unknown. Their pursuits almost seemed magical and made me eager to explore the mystical country and giant bucks that roamed in it.

The first time I saw an honest-to-God monster whitetail was on a crystal clear cold November day in 1990. Mike and I booked a deer hunt and took a week off from college classes. We drove non-stop in our dad's dark blue Chevrolet Impala for twenty-five hours from our home in Montreal to a remote area in northeastern Saskatchewan—an area only a few miles from the Manitoba border.

After the morning hunt on the first day, Mike and I took a midday drive to have a glance at the "western wilderness" we had driven so many miles to reach. I remember the day was brutally cold; the sky was clear; and the high sun reflected blinding light. We ambled down a gravel road that ran along the cattle ranch.

We spotted a big bodied whitetail buck on a tree line, bounding among a herd of Hereford cattle. The 300 pound plus deer hurtled over tree stumps and around rusty red and white cows and calves. Streams of frost exhaled from his nose and mouth at every jump. We stopped the car and watched him as he cut back and forth through the herd until he eventually cleared a five-strand wire fence, landing on the road in front of us. He stopped his gait and turned and gazed at our car with his squinty eyes. He looked like a Brahma bull in body with a massive neck, deep chest, and he carried a heavy dark rack. We both knew this was the largest whitetail we'd ever seen and a second or two later, he bounded off over the bar ditch and into spruce timber. Gone.

We hunted for a week, and saw some nice bucks, including an enormous brute moving through willows on a frozen beaver swamp. I only got a quick glimpse of this trophy deer from a very long distance. We returned home without having fired a shot on our hunt. There was no question in our minds that the Canadian Prairie Provinces were home to giant deer. We would return one day.

I believe hunting trophy whitetails in Alberta embodies the essence of fair chase. The quarry lives in enormous free-range country with endless agricultural fields and limitless forests of "crown land." Whitetails have exceptional eyesight, hearing, sense of smell, and a remarkable capacity for self-preservation. The oldest and largest bucks often live nocturnally, never to be seen during daylight hours. Population densities are low due to harsh Canadian winters and carnivorous packs of hungry timber wolves, bears, and coyotes. Provincial hunting regulations prevent hunters to bait or use mechanical feeders or shoot from vehicles. Sportsmen must wait in ambush, which means sitting for hours in a box blind or tree stand, or else stand somewhere motionless. My preferred approach is by spot and stalk: sneaking along field edges at first and last light of the day, scan and search for deer on the move, find a mature trophy, and creep within shooting distance.

Regardless of the method, the endeavor is typically done in bone chilling Arctic conditions and deep snow. I spent many days hunting in temperatures that tested my mettle at minus 40° with my fingertips, toes, and any exposed skin threatened by frostbite. To complicate the challenge of hunting these northern monarchs, the opportunity at a trophy deer might come once or not at all during a week of hard hunting, and the opportunity is likely to be a running shot at 300 yards in a blizzard. The pastime seems miserable and often it is, but when successful, the guide and hunter stand in powder snow in the gray light at the end of the day, gazing at the animal in awe of his enormous body and the heaviness of his antlers. They realize the agony of the chase, at that moment, is an easy price to pay.

ALBERTA
November 14, 1997

"On the 12th, Dave McClure killed a 172 inch 10 point with me. What a beautiful deer. The 12th was a fantastic day of hunting. We saw six bucks in the morning and killed this big one at last light behind Frank Litzes' yard pasture. A 300 yard shot put this giant down."

In August 1997, I traveled from Zimbabwe to Montréal, stopped in at the house, and said hello to my parents. I swapped my .500 Jeffrey for my .300 Mag, dropped off my safari gear, and packed my cold weather clothes. When my short visit was over, I left for northern Alberta.

By mid-November, I was enjoying a successful season. My clients took some big black bears, an exceptional moose, a couple of elk, and my first whitetail hunter shot a very old, heavy beamed nine point. All was going great.

Dave McClure of Pennsylvania arrived into camp and we talked about hunting Alberta bucks while we ate dinner prior to the first day of his hunt. Dave had hunted deer since he was a kid and told me the biggest deer he'd ever taken was a small basket racked eight point. Dave's expectations were reasonable and he understood that success might not come easy or painlessly. He wanted a crack at a big Canadian deer.

For several days, we roamed the hinterlands of northern Alberta. We drove hundreds of miles on frozen gravel roads and walked for miles along the perimeter of farm fields to check scrape lines and rubs on trees as big as telephone poles. We watched bucks chase does and watched bucks search for does. The rut was in full swing but we hadn't found a mature trophy.

One morning, I drove for more than an hour in darkness through the checkerboard of Alberta's rural township and range roads. Every few miles, I'd pass a small farmhouse with a kitchen light shining through a small window. Single cab pickups sat in driveways between snow banks, running, warming, red taillights glowing, and with steady exhaust billowing from tailpipes.

We arrived at my pre-determined spot and parked my Ford F250, then began to walk as the dawn broke over the horizon, giving us enough natural light to move along a maze of thin tree lines of tall poplars that separated various fields of canola and wheat. Our strategy was to reach a specific field tucked in far from the county road and distant from the landowner's homestead. It was a harvested field that bordered a large block of bush and beaver swamp—an ideal whitetail deer sanctuary.

Dave and I walked cautiously on the hard snow, careful to avoid stepping on fallen tree limbs and branches in our path. The brittle wood cracks like a .22 rifle shot when stepped on in sub-zero temperatures. While minding the wind, we paused to raise our binoculars to scan the fields and tree lines for a few seconds until the lenses fogged over from our frosty breath and eyeball moisture. My feet, hands, and face were cold and there wasn't anything I could do about it. To quote Pascal Benin, "It was cold enough to crack stones."

We reached the edge of the wheat field. The light was gray, but there was enough to see across the large rectangular plot of stubble. We saw from a far distance several does being chased by bucks from every possible direction. I could make out a couple of young bucks, and then spotted a big mature buck that stood and watched adolescents chase the females. I set up my shooting sticks and told Dave to get the buck in the crosshairs while I had a good look at him to ensure he was a worthy trophy. I counted ten points with good length, width, and mass. I told Dave he was a great buck and to be ready to shoot. The buck stood facing us; at my best estimate he was over 300 yards away and likely closer to 400 yards. A long and risky shot. A split second later, the big whitetail turned 180° and began to stroll calmly towards the dark timber. I knew we had no shot and no chance at the buck and told Dave to lower his rifle from the sticks.

We stood shivering among the leafless poplars and short willows with numb feet and hands, and watched the autumn mating ritual continue until the irritated does decided to leave the wheat field and enter the forest edge. It was over and we marched to the truck, longing for heat and the thermos of hot chocolate.

By mid-afternoon, we returned to the same field, hopeful that the trophy buck, or another, would make an appearance before sunset. We stood in a dark and skeletal and leafless tree line. We leaned against large poplar trees, and scrutinized the far forest edge across the stubble for the first appearance of a whitetail. Daylight diminished minute by minute and the piercing cold caused intense pain and suffering to my toes and fingertips. The moisture from my breath and snot that dripped from my nose froze in the fibers of my facemask.

Suddenly, an immature buck, a two and a half year-old, appeared on the edge of the timber. He had a small eight point basket rack and there was no need to raise a rifle on him. He meandered into the stubble, lowered his head, scratched away several inches of windblown snow, and fed on residual wheat seed. He was nervous, quickly licking grain from the hard dirt, then raising his head and scanning the field for any signs of danger. We watched the little buck feed anxiously for a time until he eventually returned to the wooded sanctuary.

With dwindling hope, Dave and I continued to glass the distant timber border. The sky was overcast and the remaining light was dismal. I recall staring at my boots while I tried to wiggle my cold toes and clenched my hands tight in my woolen mitts. Often, while standing in snow, cold and miserable, I thought to myself: *Why am I doing this? I'm freezing to death.*

Then Dave blurted, "Look at that!"

I threw up my binoculars, studied the field's edge in the direction Dave pointed, and saw a huge bodied buck step out of the black shadows and walk into the snow-covered field. As he moved directly towards us, I clearly saw his thick neck and exceptional rack. His antlers were wide and tall and I knew that he had the frame of a record book buck. I calmly told Dave to rest his rifle against the tree and place a crosshairs on the deer.

He asked me, "Is the buck a good one?"

I simply said, "Yes, you'll be happy with him."

As a guide, I learned that if I showed too much excitement prior to the first shot, the hunter might become equally, or more, excited. Sometimes clients become hysterical, their heart rate jumps to a minimum of 120 beats per second. They begin breathing heavily, start shaking, lose composure, and any ability to act rationally. Then they proceed to miss the big deer and send a bullet into the ground, or into orbit, or worse yet, fumble the shot and wound the animal.

Dave asked me again if it was a good deer and I repeated that he'd be pleased with the buck. Dave had the crosshairs on the brute, the deer continued lazily towards us and stopped. With little shooting light left, I told Dave to take his safety off and be ready to shoot when the buck turned broadside. I estimate the distance to be about 300 yards. To my surprise, the buck then turned to our left and presented a broadside shot.

I whispered, "Go ahead and take him if you're steady on his shoulder."

The rifle boomed through the cold heavy air and the buck went down. At this point, I lost my composure and shouted, "Reload and hit him again, he's a freaking giant!"

Dave got equally excited, but managed another great shot and he had his trophy.

We no longer felt any discomfort or chills as we jogged down the long field along the stubble rows to the fallen deer. He was a magnificent old buck with a very symmetrical 10 point rack and scored 172 Boone and Crockett points. Dave was overjoyed and so was I. Victory. It was a classic Canadian whitetail deer hunt.

Oversized mule deer also inhabit the broad farmland, boundless forest, and deep canyons of the Peace River country of Alberta. Like the whitetails of northern Canada, the mule deer body size increase as latitude increase and temperatures decrease. This pattern was observed by Karl Bergmann and biologically based on surface area to volume ratio and heat loss. Combine Bergmann's rule with a virtually limitless supply of a high-protein food source (such as knee deep alfalfa fields), mature muley bucks become enormous in body and antlers.

Years later, while living in South Texas, I returned annually to Alberta to guide friends who booked hunts with Mike: an Alberta outfitter and guide. Mike operates from a comfortable ranch-style house on an acreage located in a wildlife paradise that's home to whitetail deer, mule deer, moose, elk, black bear, and wolves. His property borders a waterfowl conservation area and during the pleasant months of September and October, ducks, geese, and Sandhill cranes soar overhead daily in wedge formations that resemble a sortie deployment of military squadrons. Most days, ruffed grouse peck, scratch, and gravel on his sloping driveway.

On a September morning, my good friend, Lamar Wakefield, and I prudently stalked along a sparse tree line that divided a cattle pasture and an unharvested wheat field. Daybreak brought no sun, only emerging ashen light. The air was fresh, cool, and comfortable. We heard coyotes from different directions yip, yodel, bark, whoop, cry, and howl. A couple can sound like song, but three or more resemble a symphony.

The field hardly had a flat spot and ascended from our position to a large woodlot. There were benches and shallow draws and several small poplar bluffs that stood like islands in the wheat crop. Using our binoculars, we saw bodies move throughout the field, finding small groups of muleys along with scattered single deer. For the moment, they were just bodies feeding and moving about the grain field. We needed more light to see antlers.

Several days earlier, Mike and I spotted a very good buck in this field that had excellent width and mass, and was easily identified by his long brow tines and the deep fork on his right antler. This was the buck I wanted to show Lamar.

As better light came up, we spotted some bucks and saw plenty of does and fawns. The bucks were young but the big one was absent from view or from the field. Eventually, we separated. Lamar sat on one vantage point and I on another. Apart, we could glass a much larger area, hoping to find the wide buck or another like him. After a short while, Lamar came to my position and told me, "I think I spotted the buck."

On a distant slope, not far from the timber edge, and with the Lamar's guidance, I faintly saw what looked like the tips of antlers slightly drifting back and forth among the heads of standing wheat. With my spotting scope, we scrutinized the buck further and decided that Lamar did find the buck we were looking for.

Checking the wind, we devised a plan to approach the buck to within shooting distance. Lamar was a fine shot with a rifle and shotgun, but we agreed we wanted to take the buck inside 200 yards. The closer the better. It was midmorning and the buck appeared relaxed and almost entirely hidden in the tall crop. It didn't seem like he was in a rush to go anywhere. Lamar and I crept and crawled, using the rolling contours and the sparse hardwood bluffs to camouflage our approach. Hundreds of yards later, with sore knees and hands, we reached the limit of our stalk. Lamar

Big Canadian Deer

set his rifle on my African-style shooting sticks: three pine dowels pinched at an end with a length of half-inch bicycle inner tube. Once propped, the sticks length was to serve as a rest from a kneeling or sitting position. One of the legs was broken so it was actually a wobbly bipod. With the rifle rested and the crosshairs steadied on the wheat and antler tips, we waited until the buck stood up and offered his vitals for kill shot. We waited and waited. We couldn't see the buck's eyes, but I suspect he was snoozing in his bed on that mild morning. I became impatient and decided to "make" him stand by snapping small twigs. I quietly slithered close by in the alfalfa and wheat, searching for a handful of dried and dead twigs and branches. I thought it was a better idea to alert the big muley with the sound of wood cracking by an animal breaking small limbs under hoof, than to make an obnoxious human squawk, grunt, or bellow.

The small twigs weren't loud enough, but once I bent and snapped the largest piece over my knee, the buck stood, and Lamar shot quickly and perfectly. The buck dropped as fast as he got up and disappeared in the standing wheat. We quickly scurried up to the downed buck, and immediately saw the enormous deer in body size and horns. He was bigger than we first judged and didn't suffer the awful and dreaded "ground shrinkage" that plagues the best of guides and hunters.

Lamar's magnificent mule deer was the largest bodied deer I ever guided. Back at the skinning shed, we hoisted the buck with a scale hooked to a block and tackle. Once the long deer's nose was raised clear of the concrete floor, we read his weight at 381 pounds, and in a flash the beast came crashing down to the floor.

The gambrel broke. The brute's antlers scored 201 Boone and Crockett points. An outstanding old buck.

When I reflect on the years of chasing the colossal whitetails and mule deer in the Canadian West, there is one hunt that stands out more than most, and it involved my brother Mike. As for Canadian guides, Mike has personally led hunters to more trophy deer than any guide I know. Hunting whitetails by spot and stalk is difficult anywhere, but exponentially more demanding to chase the low density deer populations north of the 55th parallel. Mike can hunt, and his hunters take great trophies.

On a November day in 1994, I was in a mule deer camp in Eastern Montana eating dinner when the phone rang. It was Mike. He was fresh out of college and guiding hunters in central Alberta, and called to tell me that he found a huge buck and his hunter came close to getting a shot at him but the buck slipped away at last light. Mike was soaring high from finding the giant, but was equally frustrated that they didn't get him. I listened to his vivid retelling of events and wished him luck to find the buck the next day.

The next evening, the phone rang, and it was Mike again. "We got him!"

That morning, a half hour before daylight, Mike and his hunter, Dennis Steffy, crept to where they'd last seen the monster buck. As sun spilled light onto the rolling grain fields and prairie woodlots, Mike and Dennis spotted three nervous does nearby, and then heard a grunt and spotted the giant buck bedded in a short clump of poplars and native grass. Dennis prepared himself for the opportunity of a lifetime. Mike blew into his grunt tube and the buck jumped up, lunged over a cattle fence, and stood broadside at forty yards. The shot was fired and a moment later, Dennis and Mike stood over one of the largest whitetail bucks ever taken in Canada during the 1994 hunting season. The monster deer scored an awesome 218 Boone & Crockett points. A buck of legendary proportions.

I've shared many successful hunts with friends and clients, and there is a unique exhilaration that guides experience when a great animal is taken. But when it came to my brother, I honestly felt more pride for Mike when he guided the "Steffy" buck than for any trophy animal I have ever guided.

I revere and respect the big bucks of Canada and I know their pursuit represents the essence of fair chase hunting. Success is hard won and comes infrequently. Deep snow, bone-chilling wind, threat of frostbite, fogged and frosted optics, deerless days, long-range running shots are all a high price to hunt the huge-bodied, heavy-antlered monarchs. But when Lady Luck shows herself, there isn't anything quite like it. Trust me.

Of Buffalo and Bullets

A hazy light broke over the horizon on a November morning in 2009. I was in Mozambique, twenty miles from the Indian Ocean. The air was stifling and sweltering heat waves flooded the vast delta. I began to sweat. I was there with a group of associates to film a buffalo hunt. My job was logistics and reconnaissance: arrange the travel and scope out camps, habitat, and animals, and drive the six-wheeled Argo.

Later that morning, we spotted a small herd of buffalo—maybe forty animals—but without any suitable bulls to stalk. By lunchtime, I was lying in tall sawgrass, eating a sandwich and perspiring in the humid, 120-degree plus temperature. I fantasied about a breeze but it never came. By late afternoon, there was still no relief from the intense heat. Our supply of water and soda was running dangerously low. While the hunting party went in search of a good bull, I decided to stay back and scout in other directions. I stood atop a six-wheel all-terrain Argo and glassed the vast landscape.

Of Buffalo and Bullets

My discomfort subsided when I spotted a cluster of cattle egrets in the distance, flapping their wings in the shimmering mirage. In this region of Africa, these crooked-neck white birds spend long hours perched on the backs of buffalo, picking ticks and parasites off their hides. Spotting these birds signals the presence of buffalo, so it was no surprise that a moment later, a herd of Cape buffalo stampeded through the papyrus vegetation. They poured out from the bright green curtain a few hundred yards away, stretching out for what seemed a mile or more. I saw bulls, cows, and calves lope and rumble in unison across the coastal delta. A stillness returned once the herd was gone. I lowered my binoculars and looked in all directions, eagerly trying to grasp the magnitude of this unique experience. I later learned that aerial surveys had counted in excess of a thousand animals in this particular herd.

The air cooled slightly as the sun no longer burned and laid low to the west. The hunting group had killed a mature buffalo bull. We butchered it and loaded the meat into the back of my Argo and then we headed back to our simple spike camp situated among tall palm trees on the edge of the delta. With a native tracker sitting next to me, I steered the slow-moving machine over the baked plain and across coastal streams as the sunset gave way to darkness. Wildfires burned in all directions. Their flames shot high into the air and danced against the black night as smoke drifted across the landscape. To me, it was an apocalyptic image that resembled oil well fires in the Arabian Desert. High above the burning grass was the Milky Way, countless stars, and the Southern Cross. This constellation is an easy find on cloudless African nights.

For hours, the Argo noisily and relentlessly jostled us along the uneven ground. Sometime before midnight, off in the distance, a gas lantern flared white, and marked the end to a grueling day in the field. I was exhausted, dehydrated, and filthy. Throughout this challenging day I had reflected on prior buffalo hunts and the great days I had spent in search of old bulls.

ZIMBABWE

July 3, 1995

Kirk and I followed up a wounded buffalo from 7:30 A.M. until 12:30 P.M. We found him bedded down and each shot it, it ran off. Followed it for several hundred yards, it was laying down, we each put two shots into it. It ran off. We followed the tracks a short ways into a thicket. The client put two shots into it, Kirk shot him, and then I shot and dropped the bull. 12 or 13 shots total. 38 1/2 inch dugga boy.

As I stood on the edge of the fire pit, staring into the log fire with a bottle of Castle Lager in my hand, professional hunter Kirk Mason appeared out of the dark with his .458 balanced on his shoulder. He joined me by the fire. Kirk told me that his party, which included his Spanish client, a tracker, and a game scout, had tracked a large herd of buffalo late in the afternoon. They reached the animals with ample shooting light remaining. A suitable old bull was spotted, approached, and shot by the Spanish hunter. A follow-

Of Buffalo and Bullets

up shot wasn't possible and the herd departed in a hurry, leaving the hunting team in a cloud of dust. Kirk's tracker, Funyan, was certain the buffalo was hit in the head or neck area. They followed the herd until dark only to find a few drops of bright red blood. It didn't look good as the wound didn't appear to be too serious.

The following morning, I stood on a hillside in waist high scrub brush, looking at a wide swath of running tracks and sporadic piles of crusted buffalo dung. Kirk asked me to join him and his client to assist in the follow-up. The Spanish hunter was a good-natured and refined gentleman, but throughout the safari, he repeatedly proved to be a poor shot. He also clearly indicated that he wanted no part of the possible mayhem the buffalo might create if we found him. He elected to follow from a safe distance with the government game scout.

There are many elements to hunting buffalo. It's about following tracks, swirling winds, and the thunderous roar of a stampeding herd. But when an old bull is spotted, everything changes. There's a unique tension and uneasiness being close to dangerous game. The final approach is cautious and calculated. There is a moment when a decision is made and rifles are raised. Adrenaline surges at the heavy fire from big-bore rifles. And finally, while the smell of cordite hangs in the air and the dust begins to settle, the internal voice in my head pleads: I hope I didn't screw up!

Sportsmen who haven't hunted buffalo may suggest, "It looks pretty simple, just walk out there and thump a bull." Granted, at times a buffalo hunt is a simple affair, but that is not always the case. The Cape buffalo might share similarities with American livestock in appearance, but it ends there. They are not an ancestor of domestic cattle. As a kid, I worked for a short time on a dairy farm and I don't remember any time that myself or any dairyman was ever charged, run over, hooked, crushed, and disemboweled by a Jersey cow. I think I'd be dead before I could jerk the teats on a buffalo cow long enough to fill a glass of milk. True, ranch hands have been injured and killed by bulls and cows in pastures and livestock pens—but it's rare. And yes, tragedies occur to young rodeo cowboys who ride for the glorified eight seconds atop a bull, bucking madly while its flank is cinched tight, but the long and short of it is: African buffalo are not the same as Herefords and longhorns. Not even close.

Tracking wounded buffalo is a perilous affair that can, in certain situations, frighten and unnerve even the most experienced hunters. Every safari season, professional hunters, safari clients, trackers, and game scouts are seriously injured or killed by ill-tempered wounded buffalo. A poorly shot buffalo quickly becomes an angry buffalo, and the follow-up is dangerous work without much of a safety net. It must be done with caution and without urgency. The hunting party must be keenly aware and focused. Unlike golf, there are no mulligans or do-overs with a botched buffalo shot.

And so, Funyan and a couple of trackers led us in the midst of the herd's swath through the low scrub. Kirk and I followed with rifles ready and carefully scanned the cover for anything big and black. Wounded buffalo often wait in ambush to deliver a menacing charge to those that inflicted the pain and hurt.

Of Buffalo and Bullets

After a short while, Funyan, found the "needle in a haystack." He spotted a single set of tracks that had split off from the herd of fifty or more buffalo. The animal's track was large and square like that of an old bull, and after cautiously following the big spoor, a drop of dark dried blood appeared in the sand. The bullet wound continued to appear minor and not fatal. We were on his tracks.

It was now midmorning and the African winter chill was gone. For a couple of hours, we moved slowly and deliberately with trackers a step in front and steady on the bull's track. Kirk and I remained alert and ready for something to happen. The lone bull took us down a shallow valley along a dry creek. There was little shaded cover anywhere in sight, but we knew this parched watershed, eventually, fed into a larger river that was flanked with large patches of thick jesse canopied by enormous trees. We were cautious at every step and collectively guessed the old boy was headed for the protective cover along the banks of the river.

Long strolls through game-rich African bush are never boring—there is so much to hear and observe: Elephants stand majestically under tall trees, flapping their giant ears to cool themselves. Bushbuck bark like dogs. Magnificent spiral-horned kudu are seen standing on a ridge, staring intently, then disappear. Big leopard tracks are temporarily followed down a game trail. A covey of crested francolin scurry into dense bush, and regal Bateleur eagles soar high above. On a rare occasion, a slithering black mamba or a puff adder is encountered. All of this activity can distract even a seasoned hunter.

We pressed on. The buffalo tracks were steady, without pause. There was very little blood, only a single drop here and there, indicating that the blood loss was minimal (equivalent to a paper cut on a human's index finger). Although we knew the trauma did not appear serious, and certainly not fatal, still, the bull was hit. Finding him was the ethical thing to do. Suddenly, the tracks vectored off course and were no longer en route to the river and the heavy cover that was a couple hundred yards straight ahead. The bull decided to change course and climb up out of the low valley, which was odd.

We continued on, stepping around noisy brush, attempting to walk softly on dried, fallen leaves. Our eyes pierced the landscape close and far, looking for the lone bull. I don't remember who spotted the tree, but I recall staring hard at a lone tree at a fair distance up the side hill. It stuck out like a beacon to me and probably did to the old bull, too. The green canopy of the single tree cast the first patch of shade from the time we picked up the tracks at first light. *Was the bull under the tree?*

Kirk and I crept along, the wind was right. Funyan led us along the tracks. The tree was a hundred yards or so to the front and the tracks headed straight for it. We stopped, Kirk and I raised our binoculars and scrutinized the shadows beneath the limbs and leaves—there he was—a big dark mass at the base of the tree. Funyan fell in behind Kirk and me. We paused for a few moments, I lifted the bolt of my rifle and slid the action back enough to see the shiny brass of the .458 round, then rechambered it, closed a bolt, and slid the safety back to "safe." Kirk did the same and decided

Of Buffalo and Bullets

the plan was to tiptoe as close as possible, and then get a shot or two into the bull before he saw us or winded us and hightailed it for parts unknown.

We bent at the waist to remain below the height of the scrub and carried the rifles in our right hands, with the left hands extended out for balance. We painstakingly took one cautious step after another. We finally reached a point about thirty paces from the buffalo under the tree. The bull was laying down and didn't seem to have an inkling we were in the vicinity. The low brush was thick; we saw the body of the buffalo, but couldn't distinguish his horns from his butt. We saw a big black "thing." It was too risky to try and get any closer, and Kirk and I determined it was best we shoot the bull as he laid in the shade of the tree. From thirty paces, we knew we could get at least two shots into him before he jumped up, and we'd attempt a couple more as he ran off. We would have to shoot through some twigs and branches, but we felt the 500 grain copper solids would hit their target. Besides, there were few other options.

I raised the Mauser, settled the white front bead in the center of the dark mass, safety off. We counted down: Three, Two, One, Fire! The big rifles boomed and I heard the solids strike. The bull got up and broke into a hard run to our left. I raced the bolt back and pushed another round into the chamber and sent another slug towards the fleeing buffalo's rear end as the bush closed in behind him.

He was gone.

Once the dust settled, we topped off our magazines and chambered rounds. We quietly walked to the base of the tree. It was obvious where the bull had been laying for many hours. A large sandy spot was bare and smooth with small dark droplets of dried blood on the outer edge of the buffalo's bed. It did appear to have a head wound, but the blood loss was minor. The bull ran off in the direction of the riverine and down the slope of the valley. Large holes in the sandy soil marked where his square hooves urgently tore at the ground after our first shots struck him. The heavy path was easy to follow through the sparse scrub. We soon found blood splattered on limbs and in his spoor. We'd hit him.

The burgundy colored blood revealed the abdominal blows. We halted on the tracks and decided to wait twenty minutes, and hoped the buffalo wouldn't run a marathon before he came to rest. We continued on, the deep tracks and blood splatters were simple to follow in the deep sand and thin brush. Kirk and I stepped softly and kept our eyes wide open, ready to respond.

Tracking wounded buffalo is intoxicating. The old warrior knows he's being followed; he's wounded and ill tempered. The outcome is unknown and the sequence of events is unpredictable. Fear is adrenaline producing. There is tension at every step, heart rates are elevated, and blood pumps fast through veins. Hunters get killed each safari season within similar scenarios.

It was midday, the sun was high, and I was hot and hungry. The trackers carried water, but food was miles away in our Toyota Land Cruiser—where we had left it five hours earlier. No lunch break. The bull led us down into the heavy jungle that coursed along the large dry river. The bull's strides shortened and the blood loss increased. I recall the tracks veered left around a thicket, and

Of Buffalo and Bullets

there, twenty paces in front of us, was the bull on his belly, laying in a small clearing, looking away from us. The big fellow was not black, but light grey. Its sparse hair covered by patches of cracked sunbaked mud. He instantly knew we were behind him and he began to get up. I managed to shoot him twice, as did Kirk. The bull never flinched—and ran off—again. I tried for his spine, but obviously missed. We slid a couple of rounds from our ammo belts and replaced the fired ones. The buffalo was very ill and likely not very far. Again, we waited a short while to let the dust settle and drank water from our canteens.

Now there was more blood to follow and the galloping bull's deep hoof prints were clear in the riverbanks' deep, soft sand. We continued cautiously for a couple hundred paces or so, and abruptly stopped when we heard a "psst." Funyan heard a sound in front of us. There were dark pockets of green bush in all directions and we gazed hard into nearby thickets. There he was. Funyan spotted the bull standing deep in the shadows of dense foliage. The old warrior's head hung low. He was sick. Kirk called back to the game scout to bring the Spanish hunter up to *coup de grace* his buffalo.

We moved in close. Kirk stood to the right of the Spanish hunter and I stood to his left. The Spaniard raised his rifle, took aim, and then the big gun thundered. The buffalo stumbled, the hunter reloaded quickly and fired another round into the bull. Surprisingly, the buffalo spun quickly. Kirk quickly fired his .458, I fired mine, and the tenacious bugger went down. It was over.

The grizzled old bull had good horns and very large bosses. I'd like to think he was courageous. The Spanish hunter was pleased, but apologized for his poorly placed shot of the previous day. The bull died hard and that's regrettable. The Spaniard's very first shot did hit the bull in the head. The slug slightly grazed the buff's forehead—just below his bosses. It was a near miss.

In 1995, I shot an elephant cow for the Independence Day celebration, and in 1997, I shot a buffalo cow for the same feast. In that span of two years, almost to the date, I'd witnessed fabulous African hunting and developed an endearment for the wild game that roam the bush veldt of Zimbabwe. I learned the ways of the African bush from professional hunters with vast experience and skill. Their professional hunter licenses are earned by passing rigorous practical hunting examinations and extensive testing of flora and fauna knowledge. Zimbabwe professionals have proved their mettle and are some of the finest guides and hunters in Africa. Since I was a Canadian expat, I couldn't obtain this enviable license.

April days are hot in the Zambezi Valley, and I recall the stillness and noontime humidity the day I shot the buffalo cow. Rarely are females taken, but the tribal council requested a cow.

Mitch Bunce (a professional hunter and good friend), several trackers, and I departed our tented camp on foot in search of buffalo. The trackers ventured off in one direction and Mitch and I in another. I remember our hunt as casual, low-pressure, and in continuous conversation: it was a nonchalant affair on a muggy April day.

Of Buffalo and Bullets

We approached a wide impenetrable thicket that began to border a narrow bone-dry watercourse we'd followed for some time. One of us (probably Mitch) heard the hissy crackling of ox peckers—red-billed ox peckers to be exact. The presence of ox peckers often equates the presence of buffalo. These noisy little birds spend time perched on various large mammals and snack on ticks, fleas, and other parasites. They certainly don't seem to bother buffalo, rhinoceroses, or antelope, and are welcomed groomers. I soon saw the ox peckers rise above the tops of the jesse and settle back down. We moved in closer and heard the grunts, snorts, and soft bellows of the buffalo. The wind was good and steady. Heavy smells of dung and musky urine wafted into us. We played cat and mouse with the herd for an hour and a half, and never saw but a patch of dark hair, dried mud, and the tip of a horn. The herd never left the security of the dense cover as they moved along the dry creek. We got close, the wind swirled, and they ran off. This happened again and again. Eventually, we stalked to 15 or so paces from the herd, and through the dense vegetation—I spotted buffalo parts and pieces.

It was time to make a move or keep forcing the herd into thicker and thicker cover. I nodded to Mitch that I'd go around the thicket in front of us and try to get a poke at one. I high-stepped quickly and quietly around the jesse and then saw, through a small opening, a complete buffalo for the first time all day. Several startled buffalo saw me, too and began to shuffle and trot. I raised my .416 and watched buffalo swiftly pass, dust was in the air. The bulls, cows, and calves crossed left to right. I wasn't about to shoot at a moving buffalo for fear of making a poor shot. Then, quite strangely, a cow entered the opening and paused just a little too long. With the rifle raised, I found her in the scope, put the crosshairs on her shoulder, and squeezed the trigger. The rifle roared and the cow fell forward. I ejected the spent casing and chambered another round, but before I could get another shot off, the cow got her legs under her and ran off.

A moment later, all was quiet. Perhaps a minute later, the cow rattled her death bellow. She did not go far. My shot was close and was later measured at 11 paces. Exciting stuff.

The trackers heard the shot and soon found Mitch and me. Additional camp staff arrived, the cow was quartered and carried out of the bush.

The Cape buffalo is the most common of the "Big Five." They are big and strong. Some find this magnificent bovine ugly, I do not. From a distance and unbothered, buffalo appear gentle and quiet. When a bull is wounded, he can be dour, vengeful, and an unmerciful terror. He is tough and can take tremendous punishment from big rifles and still press on, crush a man into the ground and kill him. But oddly, I'm addicted to buffalo hunting. It's the old bulls—the dugga boys—covered in mud and with worn broken horns that affect me to my core. I'd track a single old cantankerous nyati bull for miles and days, for the hunt and not the horns, and, ultimately, for the heart-pounding thrill.

Bears

ALBERTA

September 14, 1997

Until the 14th, I was hunting bears. Harry Schilling M.D. was in camp... Harry killed the biggest bear in the outfit's history. Squared 8'2" and weighed 575 pounds. What a bear! Took five of us to load him on the four-wheeler. He shot him with my 375/300...

The twilight disappeared; it was dark. I'd parked my Ford pickup on the slight shoulder of a long, straight gravel range road, which cut through alfalfa and wheat fields to the west and a massive wilderness of "crown" forests to the east. A mile inside the timber, my hunter, Dr. Harry Schilling of San Antonio, Texas, sat on a plywood board 15 feet off the ground in a triangulation of spruce trees. He was hunting the largest bear he'd ever seen.

The previous evening, during the last dim minutes of the hunt, a giant bear crossed in front of Harry at 15 paces. The bear ambled slowly into view and paid no attention to the bait. His head hung low; he strode on heavily muscled legs and shoulders, his gait was pigeon-toed with one paw placed slowly in front of the next. The bear's muzzle was gray; he had small, rounded ears and his black hide shook with every step. He continued quietly along the soft mossy bear trail. Harry held his bow; he knew that letting an arrow fly at a moving bear is simply reckless. The bear was gone.

The next night, I backed my Honda four-wheeler out of the bed of my pickup, down a ramp, and started into the woods to meet Harry. On this hunt, Harry decided to take my .375 along with his bow, if the big bear returned, he didn't want to lose another opportunity at the huge boar. He wanted that bear.

I meandered along the two-track path at a low speed. The Honda's headlight beamed light into the forest and reflected off the trees, brush, and tall grass. Fifty yards or so from the stand location, I stopped the ATV and shut off the engine. After 10 seconds or so of stillness, I broke the quiet and called into the pitch dark, "Harry, how was the hunt?"

Harry shouted back, "There are a bunch of bears in the trees, be careful coming in."

At the sound of the four-wheeler, small bears that had been busy feeding on the bait scampered up nearby trees. I started the Honda's engine and puttered in closer to the bait stand. I held an oversized Maglite in my left hand and began to spray the beam high into the spruce and poplar trees, looking for the bears.

Bears

Harry remained seated in the elevated stand. I continued to cast the light amid the treetops and saw several sets of shiny eyes of immature bears as they clung to tree trunks far above the timber floor. He told me the monster lumbered out in the near dark, so he decided to take the brute with my .375. He fired twice and the bear bolted off, out of sight. He soon heard loud crashes and growls. He was certain that the bear had died a short distance away.

The first splattering of blood was quickly found. Harry's aim was true and the dead bear was close by. Harry had not exaggerated; the grand old bear was gargantuan. As I stood with the surgeon from Texas, I realized I had handled over one hundred dead black bears as a guide, but never imagined that one could grow to this size. He carried a short autumn hide with even hair, his head was larger than the diameter of a basketball, and his teeth were blunt and broken and worn. He wore scars: his ears were tattered and his heavy paws were wide with strong arching claws. I didn't know his age, but guessed he was 20 years or older. He was magnificent... immense. To call him a freak of nature alludes to inferiority. This great bear was not inferior in any way.

I rode the four-wheeler back to my truck, retrieved my bag phone, and called in reinforcements. It took five men to load the beast onto the Honda. The ATV agonized under the heavy load; it overheated before it reached my Ford truck. When we eventually got to camp, it was after midnight.

BRITISH COLUMBIA
September 17, 1996

There are lots of grizzlies.

... I spotted a boar chasing two cubs and a sow up the mountain. The three bears came within 40 yards of us.... This afternoon I spotted sows and cubs. No boars. Heavy fog and rain came in and we packed it in at 4 P.M. Limited visibility gave us a hard time finding our way out. My compass probably saved us from spending the night on the mountain.

The first grizzly bear I ever saw was from the rear seat of a yellow single-engine Piper Super Cub. It was a dusky July evening and the plane droned easily over the Kluane River in the southwestern corner of the Yukon Territory. It was a light brown bear with a pronounced blonde hump above its shoulders. The grizzly didn't appear big as it sauntered along the narrow sandy strip that followed the river. The plane was low and the grizzly paid no attention to it as it continued along the water's edge. Over the next few months, I saw several more grizzlies, but the sightings were rare.

The Dease Lake Highway meanders through the Cassiar Mountains—a range of granite peaks, timber slopes and valleys, gin-clear rivers and streams, and territory that attracted gold prospectors in the 1870s. The scenery is spectacular. The drive along this hard road has little traffic with few interruptions. The small towns are modest with a roadside diner, filling station, and general store. Life is simple in this part of the world and the people are kind and inquisitive.

It was September 14 and Dave Hafer, a carpenter from Pennsylvania, arrived to base camp. We were to hunt for the next 10 days, focused on a trophy grizzly first and a black bear second. The morning of day one, we were on horseback, ascending and switchbacking a sparsely timbered slope that had been ravaged by wildfires. The wounded landscape of black bark and limbless tree trunks appeared gothic on this gray day. Once we breached the high ridge above the burn, I led our saddle horses and pack string through a forest, skirted a small mountain pond, and stopped short of the treeless alpine slopes. Camp was pitched. Our accommodations consisted of two small dome tents and a 10 x 10 blue tarp tied off at shoulder height to stunted spruce trees. My journal reminds me that I cooked us meals of pork chops, steaks, beans, potatoes, cream style corn, and slices of white bread. We drank cold water from a tin cup dipped out of a mountain stream.

We hiked along high ridges and glassed hillsides of berry bushes, distant muskegs, and lofty tundra meadows. I have a photograph of a grizzly sow sitting on her rump, her forelegs hung bent, gazing at Dave and me from a short distance. The steep slope's vegetation was brilliant with greens, yellow, and red. Her two cubs were in motion—a downhill retreat.

We saw bears every day, some big and many small. A few big bears were stalked, but not successfully. Most days it rained, but the days the sun shined were comfortable and congenial. Persistent dark days of cold, wind, and rain can drain a hunter's enthusiasm.

One day, I watched a golden eagle repeatedly swoop down, flaring its talons and wide wings to within a foot or two of the stone sheep. It was trying to force the solitary animal off a cliff and fall far below to its death. At each low-pass, the ewe rose up on her back legs and punched her front hooves towards the large eagle. The ewe stood its ground and stayed on the mountain. The eagle eventually gave up and soared into the thermals, out of sight.

By the end of day five, we counted 35 bear sightings. The country was crawling with grizzlies. On day six, we woke up to two inches of freshly fallen wet snow. By noon, all bear sightings were far below us as the new snow pushed the bears to lower elevations. We followed the bears and continued to hunt for a trophy grizzly. We sat patiently, glassed thoroughly, and stalked cautiously, but failed to connect.

On day ten—the last day of the hunt—the sky was overcast and it drizzled. My journal reads…

We cut through the burn and made our way over to the draws and ridges at the base of the mountain. We watched the wind the whole way. At 2 P.M., we found a great place to glass from. After two minutes or so we spotted a big sow and a cub. 45 minutes later I spotted our bear. These bears fed in front of us for hours. Never more than 400 to 500 yards away. The sow and cub fed out of sight. We waited till 5 P.M. watching the boar make his way towards us. A deep draw prevented us moving towards him. Finally he was about 275 yards away—a long distance for shot at a bear….

Bears

The bear was big, blocky, and mature—as large as any bear we'd seen since the first day of the hunt. We were running out of time and daylight—it was a now or nothing situation.

I had confidence that Dave could make the shot. He knew his rifle and the ballistics of this .338—he knew how to shoot. I had watched him practice at long-range targets. I told him to get a good rest and watch to get the bear in the crosshairs. In prone position with the rifle firmly secured on his daypack, Dave was rock solid on the bear. The bear casually fed and ambled closer and closer. This was it, now or never. I told Dave to push his safety off. The dark, heavy bear turned broadside and Dave's rifle roared. He fired a second shot hard after the first. The bullets struck with a thud and water flew off the bear's hide. The grizzly rolled and tumbled down the slope between the charred stumps and through berry bushes until he got traction, and then was bent on escape.

By now, the big bear, I guessed, was 200 yards away and charging uphill, tearing at the earth, reaching and pulling at the lichen-covered slope. Dave fired a third shot and anchored him to a standstill, the hollow thud of the hit echoed across the draw. The rifle boomed a fourth and final time; the big bullet found its mark and the bear went down. Dave reloaded, but watched the bear for a while. He was motionless. We worked our way quickly through the tangle and briars and over fallen trees. We reached him. He was a beautiful mountain grizzly that wore scars of a hard life eked out in unforgiving country.

We had little time, as darkness was close. We took a few photos and I skinned the bear as quickly as I could. The hide was wet and smelled like a soaked dog. After a few strokes with my knife, my hands were slimy with grease. The bruin carried a heavy layer of fat in preparation for a winter's hibernation. I crammed the heavy hide and skull into my pack frame and began to march out. We covered ground with quick steps and reflected on the last day/last hour's experience. We made it out to the trailhead with a wisp of light remaining. Ten days of hard hunting, 51 grizzly bear sightings. Classic bear hunt in the finest grizzly country.

September 24, 1996

We got our grizzly today! Last day and during the last hour of the hunt.

... We made our way over to the draws and ridges at the base of the mountain, watching the wind the whole way... I spotted our bear. He stayed in front of us for a couple of hours... The grizzly was a good boar with a big skull. Great hunt. 10 days— 51 bear sightings. Ross and I fleshed the bear after dinner. We finished at 1:30 A.M.

Monstrous bears are mystical beasts to me. Black and white photographs of Morris Talifson and Bill Pinell posed with impossibly huge Kodiak bears are etched in my mind. *How can brown bears get that big?* I've wondered. These men were pioneers in the bear hunting world; they carved out a hard living, endured nature's most rigorous hardships, and braved an outdoor life

Bears

known only to a few. They hunted the greatest and biggest bears—the Alaskan brown bear.

During several Yukon hunting seasons, I frequented a roadside diner on the boundary of our hunting area. It was a simple and remote little restaurant on the edge of a big lake. There were float planes and aluminum boats with outboard motors half-hitched and tied-off to the faded planks and posts of the wharf.

In the dining room of the restaurant, nailed to a plywood wall, was a huge brown bear hide. It was angled, all chocolate in color, it'd been hastily skinned. I don't recall if the claws were attached to the skin, but the head was tanned flat and without the typical open mouth growl commonly seen with bear rugs. The old hide was flat from nose to tail—it was humongous. I didn't think a bear could grow so big.

As with the first grizzly—the first brownie I ever saw was also from a bush plane. The bear was on the shoreline of the saltwater bay. The bear was more light in color than dark brown, likely a sow. I was on a short flight into bear camp far down the Alaskan Peninsula—a desolate wilderness jutting out long into the Bering Sea. The sky was blue and without clouds, the upper stretches of the mountains still held snow, and small streams coursed through the treeless valleys and emptied into the bay. The landscape was— surprisingly—spectacular, much more than I thought it would be. I spotted a few simple cabins along the shoreline and a moment later, the Cessna 206 with big tundra tires touched down on the narrow beach strip. I had arrived. I was in the land of the great bears.

ALASKA

May 10, 2014

Brad Brock, our guide Mark Glaser, and I are sitting on a bluff overlooking an inlet in Canoe Bay. It's opening day of bear season... We saw two small bears a couple miles away. Numerous caribou, two foxes, many bald eagles, seals, and otters. We also spotted sea ducks and some pairs of ptarmigan....

I joined Brad Brock of Houston, Texas, on his hunt. Brad is an accomplished hunter and has hunted dangerous game and has taken Cape buffalo, a big leopard, and a heavily maned lion. He decided that he wanted to hunt for a big brown bear.

Most of our first day hunting was spent sitting on moss and lichen covered rocks, leaning back against our daypacks, and glassing an enormous amount of real estate. We searched for bears along miles of beaches, expanses of alder thickets, barren alpine slopes, and along the hillsides of snow at higher elevations. More and more bears were leaving their dens after a long winter's sleep. Large holes in the snowpack on high slopes were easily seen through the spotting scope (as were the trails that traced their way down out of the snow to lower elevations to feed on berries, grass, and any prey they could catch). Springtime is also the brown bear mating season—the rut—and the big bears cruise through this Aleutian country in search of receptive sows.

The weather was warm with no rain, which was unusual on the peninsula in the springtime. Our first day of hunting produced a couple of young bears a long distance off. I've seen many red foxes in my life, but on the peninsula, these diminutive predators are curious and unafraid of humans. While glassing for bears, a couple of foxes approached to within a few paces of me.

On day two, heavy fog postponed our departure from camp until 10:00 A.M. By 1:00 P.M. Brad, our guides, Mark Glaser and Micah Ness, and I sat high on a rock formation a short distance from the bay's shoreline. The view was remarkable. Tidal flats sprawled for miles around us, alders were thick on hillsides, and a stream snaked its way through a long valley that ended at the base of a mountain, which resembled a downsized version of Europe's Matterhorn.

After surveying the vast wilderness for an hour or so, Micah, while peering through his spotting scope, calmly said, "I think I found a bear."

It was a dark spot, almost black, on the lower slope of the "Matterhorn." I barely made out the bear in my 10 x 40 binoculars, but I did see the dark form. With the help of the GPS equipped with a topographical display, it was determined the bear was four and a half miles from our vantage point. We watched the bear for some time. He was alone and moved about slowly on a high bench above a swath of alders that followed the stream. After a while, we noticed the bear hadn't moved at all for 15 minutes—he'd fallen asleep! Through the scope, the bear appeared very dark and without any light color. Mark and Micah felt confident it was, in fact, a boar. We decided to go after him.

It was 3:30 P.M. when we hiked down off the rock outcropping and started across the tidal flat. For the next six hours, we walked along bear trails on the banks of the twisting clear water stream—a stream we had carefully crossed at least a dozen times. We fought through the jungles of alders and climbed ridges every so often to check on the bear. Every time we checked, he hadn't moved at all. Halfway to the bear, I knew there was no turning back—it was late enough in the day that whatever we'd decided to do, we'd have to spend the night somewhere in the valley. Getting back to the boat and then to camp before dark was now impossible; it was tough going, but we pressed on and I grew tired.

By 9:00 P.M., we'd made it far up the long draw and were close to the base of the Matterhorn. The sun dipped below the mountain peaks; the valley was shaded and the air got cool. We climbed a low ridge to get another look at the bear before we pressed on any closer. We could see him laid out on his belly and still sound asleep. He was dark brown and we were close enough to see that he was a big mature bear. We crossed the fast-flowing stream one more time and climbed a steep slope. We pulled and fought through the unforgiving alders until we reached the tundra bench several hundred yards from where we'd last seen the bear.

At this point, we dropped our packs and Brad and Mark checked their .375s and made sure they were loaded. I carried shooting sticks and Micah filmed the stalk. We eased our way around alder patches, cautiously placing our feet to avoid breaking a branch or a small limb. The wind was steady and perfect. If the bear got our scent, the six-hour plus stalk would be for naught, as the bear would run over a mountain and out of the valley. We continued slowly, the shooting light darkened.

Bears

Suddenly, the bear appeared a couple hundred yards straight ahead of us. No longer asleep, he was moving and he was huge. I quickly placed the shooting sticks in front of Brad and he settled his rifle into the V notch. The bear moved behind some alders and then ambled into a low spot and went out of sight. Brad grabbed his rifle, I gathered the sticks, and Mark led us forward. We were bent at the waist and swiftly stepped to close the distance to the bear.

Without warning, the bear's head appeared and then the rest of him rose out of a shallow draw. The big bear was about one hundred yards from us. I put the shooting sticks out, Brad returned his rifle to rest in the notch, got his head down on the stock, and put the crosshairs on the massive bear. He had a huge hump above its shoulders, heavy muscular legs, and a giant head. The bear knew something was up—maybe he had heard us. The wind was still steady and in our favor. He stopped, stared in our direction, and then began to lumber towards us. Mark whispered to Brad that he was a good bear and to wait until he presented a broadside shot. I recall the bear turned to our left and then to back to our right. Brad was on the bear, the brownie stopped, stood broadside, and then the big rifle roared.

The impact of the bullet into the heavy hide was easy enough to see. Brad hit the bear perfectly in the shoulder. He reloaded and sent along another shot. The monster bear began to roll down the gentle slope to our right, crashing through alders and growling as he tumbled. Mark and Brad moved in front of me and towards the wheeling bear. Brad's .375 boomed again as he poured another shot into the bear. The brown bear came to rest against heavy alders.

Brad and Mark moved in close with rifles ready. From 30 feet away, Brad fired a final shot into the massive animal. He had his trophy.

The bear was a true Goliath—everything about him seemed oversized and imposing. I've guided hunters to seven and eight foot bears, but they were small compared to this brute. I felt a profound elation and was thrilled for Brad and for all of us who had endured the arduous hike over difficult terrain. Brown bears commonly live for twenty-five years and Brad's bear was likely over twenty and he was magnificent.

May 12, 2014

Brad shot his monster bear last night! Yesterday, due to morning fog, we left camp at 10 A.M. We climbed a lookout point close to the beach…. Mike and I spotted a bear 4.5 miles away. It was at the base of the mountain that resembled the Matterhorn. We decided to go after the bear….

…. The bear was shot at 10:10 P.M. We finished getting him skinned by 1:15 A.M. We stayed under alders along the stream. Quite miserable! It was cold and damp with misting rain. We made a fire at 4:30 A.M. and left when we had enough light to see—about 6 A.M. Got to the boat at 11 A.M. Absolutely sore, hungry, and exhausted. The tide went out and the boat was on dry ground. We slept on the beach until the tide came in. Incredible hunt…

For me, there are few animals that intensely evoke such awe, respect, wonder, and fear as a huge brown bear. Stalking these giant bears in the magnificent and wild country of the Alaskan Peninsula ranks as one of the finest experiences anywhere in the world. Brad's great bear measured 10'4" and had a 28 5/16" skull. A truly spectacular specimen.

Our Lion

June 16, 1997

Mike and I killed a lion yesterday! Mike's fourth day in Africa and his first kill is a 9'3" male lion. Not a bad start....

I grabbed the .416 and told Albert to switch on the light. Looking them over quickly through the scope, put crosshairs on the lion-high shoulder shot and squeezed off. Down he went. Dust cleared, Mike clobbered him with the .458 and then I fired once more. He never went anywhere... The cat was now dead. We loaded the lion with the lioness 150 paces away. We paraded amongst the villagers —women shouting, singing and dancing. Never seen natives so festive...ever!

I stood in the reception area of the Bulawayo Airport and looked through the windows into the Customs and Passport Control area. There he was, my brother Mike, getting his passport stamped.

Our Lion

Finally, Mike was in Africa. He'd come to visit his big brother and get a taste of safari life. Little did he know that while he was flying half way around the world, lions were causing problems in one of the safari company's hunting areas. Marauding lions were killing cattle, goats, and sheep.

Once Mike's duffle bag was secured in the Toyota, we drove north towards the Zambezi Valley. Mike was a seasoned traveler in the United States and Canada, but Africa was completely foreign. He looked at everything and everyone we drove past, marveling at all that was new to him. Countless Zimbabwean men walked along the highway. Native women who balanced bundles of firewood or water jugs on their heads followed the men. Barefoot children in ragged clothes followed their mothers. Rib-thin, tan-colored dogs were seen in every direction, walking, sitting, and standing around thatched native huts clustered in the barren dusty landscape. Eventually, the countryside became softer with impeccably manicured farms with rows of gum trees that lined the entrances to the colonial estates. These very farms employed the natives and were the food source of the nation.

I remembered that we traveled through Gweru and most likely stopped in Kwe Kwe for a meat pie and a Coke. A few miles north of Kwe Kwe, we turned west and drove the remaining one hundred or so miles through *communal lands*. We arrived to "Main Camp" by nightfall.

Reports were delivered daily for more than a week prior to Mike's arrival to camp. The reports consisted of handwritten letters that described the problems at hand, along with locations and requests that these incidents be investigated. Along with the lions, other common problems included elephants that destroyed maize fields or pushed over elevated grain bins, spilling a season's worth of harvest. Buffalo bulls were invading cotton fields and eating the crop. Leopards killed livestock, too. Of these, the elephants and lions were most problematic.

The safari company's staff was not only responsible for investigating the reports, but the staff members were also there to help the villagers with the problem-animal issues. Often, the best and only solution was to shoot the animal. Under certain circumstances, an alternate option to shooting was figuring out a way to force the animal(s) back into a nearby game park or hunting area.

I remember a certain nuisance elephant I once stalked in a standing maize field. The bull was continually raiding a villager's crops and had to be dealt with in some fashion. I approached from a suitable distance to shoot the bull, with every intention to kill it, but the heaviness of killing another elephant forced me to reconsider shooting the old tusker. Albert, my tracker, was close behind with a 12 gauge pump shotgun. I swapped my .500 Jeffrey for the shotgun and then shot the bull, peppering him with #8 birdshot in his rear until the gun was emptied of shells, and then chased him for a mile or so back into the sanctuary of a nearby game park. The elephant lived another day. He was likely annoyed at the mild stinging of small pellets striking his heavy hide. For reasons right or wrong, I just didn't want to kill an elephant that day.

The current reports were from our southern hunting area in the vicinity of the Lutope River and Sengwa River, which bordered

Our Lion

the Sengwa Research Area. Mike and I packed up supplies in the Toyota and headed south. Driving in the tribal lands of Africa is a miserable affair. Roads are deep in fine dust. The jarring and vibration experienced from skimming and banging over the ruts is enough to loosen fillings. Roads pass through the middle of villages and not around them. Goats have the sense to avoid oncoming traffic, but donkeys just stand in the way, bringing vehicles to a complete stop. As bad as it is traveling through rural Africa, it is wonderful to see the smiling and laughing children as they rush towards our moving truck—they wave both hands and shout: "Hello, Hello!"

After two hours of horrible driving conditions over dusty, washed out roads, we finally arrived at the Chirisa Safari Area headquarters. We met with Senior Ranger Maroki, discussed the lion problems, and presented the reports I had received. In this area, to shoot a problem lion, required written permission. Within a few moments, I was granted permission and was handed an official permit to shoot a lion.

Next stop was our safari camp located on the banks of the Manyoni River. The simple camp consisted of three olive-colored safari tents and a dining tent. It was reminiscent of camps from the 1930s and 40s: the "Golden Age" of East African safaris. It was a delightful spot with towering acacia trees that shaded the campsite from the daytime African sun. The camp's primary purpose was to accommodate company staff who were conducting problem-animal work in the area, or were there to hunt game entering the hunting area from the bordering research area. In this hunting block, safari clients took heavy-tusked elephants, some old buffalo bulls, the occasional leopard, but virtually no antelope.

Mike and I spent a couple of days driving from one village to another checking on the reports. We looked for fresh lion sign, spoke with farmers, villagers, and a few local chiefs as we tried to get an idea where the lions were located. All the evidence (tracks and kills) showed, at a minimum, to be a week old. The lions had come and gone.

After futile attempts to locate the whereabouts of lions residing in the communal lands, I decided to pay a visit to the Sengwa Research Area. At the time, the area was a protected reserve for animal study and granted access solely to wildlife biologists and Zimbabwe National Parks officials. I knew the head ranger in command of the research area and asked for a favor. Soon after, Mike, a couple of park rangers, and I were exploring some of the finest game country in Zimbabwe. We saw lots of game, untroubled and unafraid. The park's two-track meandering bush road took us close to huge herds of elephants, hundreds of buffalo, greater kudu, zebra, impala, warthogs, waterbuck, leopard and lions tracks—it was one helluva jaunt.

Once the tour ended, I decided to look into another problem animal report. We drove to a township situated along the Sengwa River, which was a couple of miles from the research area boundary. We were told that lions had been in the area for several days. The local school was closed and the villagers were living in fear. It was also reported that donkeys were killed during the previous night. We were brought to the kill site where we saw two dead donkeys

Our Lion

laying side-by-side, their twisted remains with dull, lifeless eyes, bodies raked with claw marks, and deep bites about their necks. It was obvious they were killed in the last twenty-four hours. One of the beasts was partially eaten on a flank, and the other was untouched. Tracks showed two lions had killed the burros. This was it—we were going after one of these lions.

We were now waiting for the lions. Mike and I sat on a bench in the back of the Toyota with our loaded big bore rifles leaning against the roll bar, binoculars hung from our necks. Albert and a second tracker, Didmus, as well as a government game scout named Christmas, sat behind us. The truck was positioned in the middle of a fallow field. Acacia limbs were hacked, cut, and removed from a nearby thicket and placed all around and on top of the vehicle. The truck was skillfully turned into a lion blind. The two donkeys lay 80 yards or so in front of us.

The African sun had set and the air was cool—it was winter. There were native mud and thatched roofed huts in all directions— evening fires glowed, mopane wood burning smoke drifted all around. The smell of mopane wood smoke is unique and always tells me I am in Africa. We heard the Tonga villagers singing, chanting, and beating their drums. The festive nature of the locals astounded Mike.

The night sky darkened and the shooting light faded. Two very drunk men decided to stroll by the carcasses. They were completely oblivious that their evening moonlight walk was at the exact time that a lion or leopard hunter calls "prime time." The brave gentlemen carried chibuku beer in football-size brown plastic jugs.

Chibuku is a wild home-brew: a fermentation derived from cooking corn, sorghum, and, sometimes, milk. This opaque intoxicant, also commonly known as scud, is the signature beverage of choice for beer drinkers in the communal lands of Zimbabwe. I've never sipped this chunky, foul-smelling beer for fear the alcoholic effects could lead me to blindness or a slow death.

Once the men in stupor were very near our truck/blind, they pleaded for us in their native tongue to shoot the evil lions and to return peace and safe living to their homes.

I responded that we'd try our best to rid their township of the cats. I then cautioned them that the lions were likely nearby, and they should get out of the area quickly. They walked away, talked incessantly, entered a nearby village, and gathered with more plastered buddies to drink more grotesque ale and to keep talking, I'm sure.

I had investigated reports of lions killing livestock many times and made serious attempts to shoot problem cats, but I'd never succeeded. Typically, lions that prey on livestock: cows, donkeys, goats or sheep—tend to relish the domestic meat and become a serious nuisance to the owners of the animals, bringing fear to men, women, and children in the local area.

Naturally, the native owners of mauled livestock often take matters into their own hands and attempt to kill lions by various methods. The lions have learned that returning to a kill in the communal lands may result in being poisoned or getting a limb caught in a snare, hence, they very rarely return to domestic animal kill, making the task of killing a livestock-killing lion very difficult.

Our Lion

By now, we were without any natural shooting light, and it was the moon and starlight that kept the sky from being pitch black. As time passed into the evening, I grew tired and departed from vivid readiness. My head dropped and I entered the early stages of sleep. While in my state of semi-consciousness, Mike declared, "One just showed up."

I asked in disbelief, "A lion?"

Mike replied, "Yes, one is at the donkeys."

I looked over at Mike staring through his binoculars, and then decided to do the same. Mike was right, the lion was easily seen in the moonlight. As the cat stood by the carcasses, a moment later, a second lion showed up. We looked over the two big cats, and I distinguished the male from the female. The male lion had a short, scruffy mane. I was going to shoot him. My National Parks permit stated only one lion to be shot: male or female. I let Albert and Didmus know that the lions were at the donkey carcasses and told them to get ready with the spotlight. Didmus was to connect the wires to the battery and Albert to shine the million candle power beam at our target.

I grabbed my .416 and Mike got hold of the .458. We glassed the lions once more and agreed which one I would shoot. "You follow-up immediately with a back-up shot," I told my brother.

I brought the rifle to my shoulder, looked through my scope, and then, for some odd reason, my heart began to beat so hard I could hardly breathe. I was falling apart and at a damn crucial moment.

Mike looked over at me and asked, "What are you doing?"

I snapped back, "Shut up, I need a second." I looked away from the feeding lions, took a few deep breaths, returned to peering through my scope, and easily identified the slightly larger male. "He's on the right," I told Mike.

Then I spoke to Albert who was sitting behind me, "Vala lo light!" (Turn on the light!)

The big spotlight beam hit those cats and made the tawny-colored hides shine, while their eyes reflected like green lasers. The male stood broadside and right of the lioness. I centered the crosshairs high on his shoulder and squeezed the trigger. The 400 grain soft point hit him hard and he tumbled, snarling and grunting. The .458 boomed next to me. I followed up with another shot and Mike did the same. The lion was down. We couldn't see him clearly due to the high grass, but we could hear him snapping his jaws and growling.

The villages around us became quiet. No doubt the locals heard the shots from a long distance. The villagers close-by likely saw the spotlight beam and heard the lion making a lot of noise after the shots began. Mike and I reloaded our rifles, did some back-slapping, and discussed our next move, which was to advance to the downed lion.

The lioness stayed very close to the lion. She was clearly more concerned about her mate than the shooting, the light beam, or the commotion. Approaching the downed lion on foot in the dark would have been foolish and dangerous; chancing a wounded lion charge or attack from the lioness crouched only yards away from her livestock-killing mate. The lion had been still and quiet for quite some time—perhaps 15 minutes or more. I wasn't certain if he was dead or alive.

Our Lion

A decision had to be made: *Who was going to drive the Toyota?*
I wanted to have the rifle in my hands upon approach, but I had a
dilemma: Didmus didn't know how to drive; Albert, if he drove,
claimed he'd be frightened at the thought of the cat jumping in the
cab if it was still alive; Mike had never handled a right-hand drive
vehicle with a manual transmission. The last thing we needed was a
driver error due to a massive panic attack on approaching a possibly
still-living lion! I decided to drive.

As I slowly drove towards the lion and donkeys, Mike stood in
the bed with the .416 rifle held firmly in his hands, Albert shined
the spotlight and Didmus sat next to me inside for reasons of self-
preservation, I suppose. At about five paces, we saw the lion lying
in the grass—he was alive. His jaws were popping and he stared
into the light.

"Shoot him!" I shouted.

Mike did—and the ordeal was over.

At about 25 paces, we saw the lioness laying on her belly,
eyes glaring at us, and her tail flickering back and forth above
the grass. She was an intimidating sight to say the least. She was
too close for us to get out of the truck and load the dead lion into
the bed. My brother and I changed places. Mike drove the truck
towards her while I stood in the bed this time with the rifle in my
hands. As Mike honked the horn, I fired a shot in the air while
the others in the truck shouted at her to move off. We eventually
succeeded in pushing her off to a distance that gave us some
reasonable safety to load the lion. I stood in the bed and aimed
the rifle at the lioness, illuminated by the truck's headlights,

while Mike and the boys heaved the lion into the truck bed. We departed.

Typically, when an elephant is killed by a hunting client, the local chief and villagers are informed. The meat is distributed amongst the people living in the district. If the dead elephant is close to the local villages, then the men, women, and children walk to the kill site and assist with the butchering of the animal. Once the locals show up, the party begins. For Zimbabweans living in tribal lands, regardless if a dead elephant was crop raider or a trophy bull taken by a hunter, it is one huge pile of much needed protein for meat-starved Africans.

As we drove into the township with the dead lion in tow, it looked like we were approaching a Mardi Gras party of near madness proportions. Young and old, male and female were dancing, singing, shouting, and laughing. I'd never witnessed such an emotionally-charged display of sheer joy in my life. Even the shy, reclusive elder women were jiving and hand-clapping among the energy charged masses. As I was slowly driving through the crowds, careful not to run over someone, streams of people approached the Toyota to see the dead lion and thank us for removing "the devil" from their community. For many days, locals had lived in fear of being attacked by the cats, schools were closed and people stayed close to their huts and villages. The township residents had been paralyzed and now were free to carry on with their daily activities and live without fear. The lioness, undoubtedly, would return to the research area to join her clan. She was never seen again.

Our Lion

Mike and I talked about the events over and over as we drove back to camp. I remember feeling an incredible sense of accomplishment—from start to finish, all aspects of the lion hunt seemed to be done right and well. The lion was taken and nobody got hurt in the process. Once in camp, we enjoyed a good meal and several cold beers and, of course, discussed every aspect of our 'triumphant feat" into the night. It was quite late when we finally retired to our tents.

I want to be clear, shooting a lion from the protection of a truck at night in the beam of a spotlight, in my opinion, is not fair-chase hunting. It's not sport, it's just shooting. An ethical lion hunt is done from the ground in daylight. The lion that Mike and I shot was a livestock-killer. The lion and lioness were a threat to the lives of men, women, and children; they had to go. Taking this lion was not a *true* hunt in the sense of the word, it was work. It needed to be done.

The future of lion hunting is plagued with uncertainty. Some hunting blocks have marginal lion populations where few lions are hunted if any at all, and other areas are overpopulated with prides of the great cats. There are biological, human encroachment, habitat loss, financial and ethical issues of lion hunting and management that require significant thought and deliberation. Sound wildlife management must prevail to ensure the survival of the magnificent African lion.

I support lion hunting and feel that shooting old males in no way harms lion populations. Scientific research and data has clearly shown that old lions pushed from prides no longer breed females. The African lion deserves our attention and respect. It would be a tragic loss if hunters and non-hunters alike of future generations could not experience lions in their wild natural habitat.

I have no interest in shooting another lion—one is enough. Hunting lions is a fascinating endeavor and can be incredibly exciting. They are magnificent creatures that symbolize Africa. The events on that cool June evening in 1997 was a defining moment in my hunting career, and to have shared them with my brother, Mike, made it all the better.

The Poetry of Shooting Quail

The first bobwhite quail I ever saw was in a swampy hardwood creek bottom in central Georgia. What I *actually* saw was totally out of focus and moving very fast.

Late one afternoon on a November day, my co-worker and hunting buddy, Chuck Humphrey, and I followed an orange and white setter named Lady. She was an easy dog. She worked through the decaying knee-high grass and briar tangle with caution and purpose. After a short time, she slowed her pace, put her head up, took a few cautious steps, and went rigid.

"Looks like she found the *burds*," Chuck said.

We moved in quickly with shotguns ready, and without advanced notice, an explosion detonated. A hundred brown buzz bombs (likely a typical bevy of 12-18 quail, but it seemed like more) flew at all angles, cork-screwing through the oaks and, finally, flared in a thicket of young planted pines. The birds were gone. It happened so fast. Chuck fired a shot and killed a bob. I soon realized I didn't fire a shot or even mount the gun. I stood like a lost child in a shopping mall, looking around at the trees as if they were strangers. I wasn't sure what to do next. The quail scared the hell out of me, and I recall being embarrassed and in awe. I'd been hunting all my life and had shot a lot of game. I'd killed little harmless finches and angry elephants, but wild quail were a new, bewildering, and just a far different "bundle of feathers." At that moment, I *wanted* to be a quail hunter.

I am often asked, "What is your favorite hunt?" Usually, the question is asked by novice hunters or people who have never hunted. Choosing a favorite hunt is like choosing a favorite book or movie, different circumstances will evoke different answers. Hunting big game is a different experience from a bird hunt—they are not comparable. My personal experiences often dictate my response: "I love to track old buffalo bulls," or, "I particularly like hunting big Alberta whitetails." Some of my most memorable days afield come to mind like short films that feature majestic animals and spectacular landscapes.

At times, I thought that there was no finer animal to hunt than the elephant. Hunting these mammoths normally requires many days of tracking, including walking for miles and miles under a burning African sun. When you finally close in—25 yards or less— to a herd of these giants, you must then cautiously search for the bull with the biggest ivory. Make no mistake…this is intense…you feel the blood pulsing in your head. This is exciting stuff…and arguably, reckless.

The Poetry of Shooting Quail

Other favorite experiences were times and places where I could watch the big sky sunsets over the golden prairies in western Saskatchewan after a day of hunting Hungarian partridge. There I witnessed waterfowl fill the sky more than any other place on earth. With shotgun cradled, I walked among the abandoned homes and barns of century-old homesteads. These places humbly remind me of my comfortable life as compared to the first settlers who lived off the land and survived the bitter Canadian winters in this raw and immense landscape. My country of birth is alluring and vast.

I often choose to hunt alone, but most memorable days afield are spent with family and friends. Whether it's shivering in a duck blind on the Ottawa River in Quebec; laughing and drinking gin and tonics around a fire in Mozambique after a day of stalking buffalo; or watching swarms of doves flying overhead while standing on a hillside in Argentina. The moments created with hunting companions while in pursuit of the wild experience create memories difficult to describe with words.

But I do have a preference. If I could only hunt one game animal, I'd choose the bobwhite quail.

The only upland birds I saw while growing up and hunting in Quebec were partridge (ruffed and spruce grouse) and woodcock. I never crossed paths with a quail. As a teenager, Robert Ruark introduced me to quail hunting in his stories of hunting with the "Old Man." He wrote about bobwhites with reverence and respect. He also called them "brave" and they were to be treated as "gentlemen." Other great writers such as Nash Buckingham and Archibald Rutledge taught me more about the little bird, and they skillfully depicted the glory of hunting *partridges* in the South. I learned that in the "old days," wealthy plantation owners and their guests followed the dogs (braces of pointers or English setters) through their pine and wiregrass forests from atop mule-drawn wagons and Tennessee Walking horses. Southern quail hunting roots are steeped in aristocratic tradition unique only to the "prince of game birds."

GEORGIA

December 10, 1998

Shot my first wild quail today. Chuck and I drove out to the Lower 500 to try to find the covey that was seen. We started with the sorghum patch...

Rocky and Judy worked beautifully and locked on point. We walked in and the covey exploded—I knocked one down on the first shot and missed the second....

It was a hen, hit her hard, and I blew her up....

It was warm day and the sun was lowering. Chuck Humphrey and I finished our work for the day. We decided to leave the plantation office, load some dogs, and squeeze in a quick hunt before dinner with our families. We chose a small milo patch that was bordered by towering white and red oak trees. Quail feed late in the day and we figured we had a decent chance of finding a particular covey we'd seen before. We parked the truck a short

The Poetry of Shooting Quail

distance from the sorghum, and turned the dogs out. With loaded shotguns, we followed the bird dogs, Rocky and Judy, into the cover. They worked into the wind, loping slowly through the knee-high crop, crossing back and forth.

Suddenly, the liver and white colored pointers went on point. Neither honored their brace mate—both were pointing. These old-timers had long-lost the style of their youth, and now showed their age: grizzled faces, drooping tails, and big ugly warts. Chuck and I moved in ready for the eruption and I prayed not to miss. The dogs had the covey pointed perfectly. They flushed directly in front of us, unobstructed, and in a fanned formation. It was a pretty sight.

I picked out a bird and squeezed the trigger and down came my first bobwhite. I cannot recall if Chuck connected, but I'm sure he did. He is a passionate bird hunter, a superb shot, and he rarely missed with his trusty 20 gauge pump. My bird was a hen and there was not much left of her (definitely not enough to eat). I'd blown her to pieces; but I had my first *wild* quail and it was cause for celebration. I was a quail hunter.

In the South, quail hunting and bird dogs go together like biscuits and gravy. Some hunters feel it is a sin to shoot quail without a dog, and hunting quail without bird dog is difficult at best. And yes, shooting the magnificent bobwhite over dogs is preferred, if not, downright mandatory.

Only a day after taking my first quail, I wanted to own a bird dog. I worked and lived on a commercial hunting preserve (plantation) and had the fortune to have access to thousands of acres of manicured quail hunting grounds. From October until March, the plantation clients shot pen-raised quail, pheasant, chukars, and some mallard ducks. There were always birds to find so I had the ultimate dog training paradise.

Jasper was my first bird dog and he was a pointer. I like English setters, German short-haired pointers, and Brittany spaniels, but the pointer is the breed that drew my attention. Pointers are lean, muscular, and have a reputation to be stubborn and hard to "break." They might be considered "pets," most are not. They are bird hunting machines. The great pointers dart through bird country with vengeance and speed with their tails cracking left-right-left-right like a violent pendulum. When they reach distant "birdy" objectives, they're found on point with head held high, inhaling quail scent, and standing tall and rigid with a poker straight tail. Pointers are determined; they have impeccable style. I wanted one.

Six-month-old Jasper came from Eddy Smith, a successful breeder, field trailer, and family friend from East Texas. The liver and white pointer had a champion pedigree and a desire to run fast and far away. Training my young pup put me through a learning curve that was difficult, frustrating, hateful, depressing, and maybe even suicidal. Eventually, the process became joyful and rewarding. Disorder became order, disobedience transformed to obedience, and chaos became control. On the days I was out of the office to guide hunts, my young dog hunted well for the plantation clients and handled quail, pheasants, and chukars with proper manners and confidence. By the end of

The Poetry of Shooting Quail

Jasper's first bird season, he was a broke dog and shooting birds over him was magical.

More pointers followed Jasper. I had dogs named Dixie, Daisy, Son, Abbey, and Robin. All my dogs were born in Texas and pointed quail on a Georgia plantation. I soon began field trialing and made friends with the best bird dog trainers in the Southeast.

The New Year's Eve blizzard of 2000 was a monster and I drove through it—from Central Georgia to North Texas. I white-knuckled the most treacherous road conditions I'd ever seen, which were worse than anything I ever experienced growing up in Canada. (Could it be a couple of years of Deep South living caused me to lose my Arctic wasteland driving skills?) The interstates and highways were covered with knee-deep snow mixed with ice. Mile after mile, in the road ditches and embankments, tractor-trailers were jackknifed and flipped over on their sides. Several kenneled pointers were curled up and shivering in the bed of my truck. We were headed to a ranch in North Texas: Eddy Smith's sprawling quail lease along the banks of the Red River. I wanted to see Jasper run hard, wide, and point wild bobwhites in Texas; but first, I had to get through the epic storm.

After twenty hours of overwhelming stress, I reached my destination. For three days, Jasper and I hunted in snow and ice, running through frozen brush and over rocky ground. Afterward, Jasper was in rough shape and needed rest. The pads of his feet were sore and worn badly. Dark blood dried to his head, legs, feet, and chest. The end of his tail looked like a cherry popsicle. I watched Jasper hunt and move through the Rolling Plains ranch like he owned it. He worked into the wind, crested distant ridges, investigated plum thickets, and searched for quail in dense oak and mesquite mottes. Each time I walked in on Jasper's staunch points, wild bobwhites erupted all around us. He found and handled quail like a pro.

Back at camp, Eddy declared to the fellow trainers, bird hunters, and field trailers that my young dog was a "brag" dog! The grueling expedition from Georgia to Texas was worth every hellish mile. Jasper proved to be the "real deal."

———————————

In 2002, our Georgia days were numbered and soon to be over. The big plantation became a bigger land deal and the groomed quail fields, hardwood bottoms, piney woods, and bass ponds were plotted into "ranchettes." Paradise lost. The wiregrass, broom sedge, lespedeza, partridge peas, and long-leaf pines are synonymous with the Southern quail experience of Georgia; but mesquite, croton, ragweed, and sunflowers of Texas "scream" quail! It was time to move the family to Texas.

By June of 2004, I'd persuaded the family to become South Texas ranchers. We vacated in-law rich and comfortable East Texas to the prickly, desolate, and unpeopled brush country of South Texas. We set up shop in what we called on the heat stroke 105 degree plus days: "the nothingness."

The rains of 2004 had exceeded those of 2003 and so did the quail hatch. There were quail everywhere. After my work duties

The Poetry of Shooting Quail

were done for the day, parents and kids routinely loaded into the Kawasaki Mule and cruised the ranch.

The summer evenings in South Texas are special—especially in the years of good rainfall. When the air cools, the setting sun casts brilliant colors against the harsh wilderness. The country is rich in wildlife. Cottontail rabbits dart back and forth across the roads. Mourning doves fly in every direction. Does and fawns feed and show little fear at passers-by, and whitetail bucks are seen briefly as they bound into the black brush and mesquite. Big rattlers slither slowly or coil tight. Bobcats and coyotes are wary, but often stand long enough for a good look and then they're gone.

Our main purpose on the meandering ranch roads was to find quail. Our passing ATV startled and flushed coveys of tiny baby quail, which were barely able to fly. Families of juveniles were seen everywhere—they ate and moved nervously along the ranch roads and trails. I never grew tired searching for quail and always savored the sight of this little bird.

As much as I enjoyed *seeing* quail, I did like shooting them. They are fast and challenging targets. At some point during my hunts, I'd filled my game vest with enough quail, and then became far more interested in finding quail than shooting them. That's when I opted to guide hunts rather than be the *guided*.

I can vividly recall my stint as a quail guide like it was yesterday. It goes like this:

My day starts in the dark. An hour or more before sunrise, I'm at the kennel, loading the rambunctious pointers, setters, and English cockers into the dog boxes on the quail truck. I check all my gear and supplies: vest, blaze orange cap, whistles, snake boots, collars (electronic and tracking), dog water, and drink cooler. I then drive to the lodge always in time to have breakfast with the three or four clients booked for the two-day hunt. Once bellies are filled up on eggs, tortillas, bacon, fruit, juice and coffee, the hunters meet at the truck, fill their vests with shot shells, and slide their shotguns (mostly twenty and twenty-eight gauge doubles) into the felt-lined custom scabbards, and climb up on the high rack bench above the dog boxes.

The quail hunt officially starts as I drive off from the lodge. The air is cool and crisp, the sun is rising slowly. The breeze is from the southeast and there is light dew on the grass—perfect conditions. The first covey of the day is the relief valve—the pressure is off. One dog is rigid on point and its brace mate is backing 20 paces away. The truck comes to a stop. The hunters climb down off the truck, retrieve their guns, drop shells into their dark-chambered barrels, and approach the dog on point. I instruct the hunters to flank the dogs and walk past them until the birds flush. The hunters listen to me. They march past the pointing dog, then suddenly, the sound of drumming wing beats causes them to instinctively mount guns. Twelve to fifteen bobwhites unexpectedly blast upwards and away, twisting and diving through the mesquites like fighter jets in combat. Shots are fired, I see a puff of feathers and a bird goes down. This is it—my moment of truth. It's like a scene from a John Cowan painting. I'm smiling and I'm "in the zone."

The hunters are laughing and cussing and smiling, too. I gather the pointers and secure them with chains on the side of the quail truck. The cockers are turned out to find the fallen birds and chase down the fleeing cripples. At this point, I decide to hunt down a single or two or move on to find another covey. Three birds taken from a covey—never more.

This scenario repeats itself all day long and I don't tire from it. Dead quail gather in the blue plastic milk crate that sits atop the dog boxes behind the high-rack bench.

The sun starts to set and casts long shadows over the South Texas prairie. Thirty minutes of daylight remains and I decide the hunt is over. The scattered quail need to find one another, and form their protective circular roost and settle in for a good night's rest. My content clients have bagged near limits of quail. They generously praise my dogs, the ranch, and the regal little bird. I drive up in front of the lodge. The hunters stiffly step down, slowly pull their quail guns from the scabbards, thank me for a memorable day in the field, and disappear into the "big house" for pre-dinner cocktails. The hunters are tired and so am I.

After a hard day of running in front of the truck, searching only for quail, the dogs are tired and curled up tight in the boxes—sleeping. As I arrive at the kennel, the dogs awake and I open the aluminum dog box doors, slip my fingers under their collars, and gently lower them down. They're returned to their kennels for much needed rest and recovery. They show cuts, scrapes, and bloody tails, but nothing serious or concerning. The wounds are temporary tattoos showing their instinctual thirst to find upland birds. The bird dogs hunted hard for me and go back to sleep.

In the good years, the dogs will point twenty, sometimes thirty, plus coveys a day. In bad years, we don't hunt quail at all.

I'm alone, drinking a cold beer as I clean quail. I snip off heads, legs and wings. I peel and strip the skin and feathers. Most of the birds are cold, but some are still warm. I examine their wings, two-thirds of the bobwhites are juveniles and the rest second year quail—a good sign of multiple spring and summer hatches. The plump white carcasses fill zip-lock bags and go into the game cooler. My day is over and I want to do it again and again.

Why my obsession with this diminutive game bird?

There are many reasons. It's the bird's poignant history, scarcity, speed, and beauty. It's the bird dogs and the covey rises, and the cool crisp mornings. It's the anticipation, the harsh and beautiful habitat, and the long casts and great finds. It's the double guns, and the great shots and inexcusable misses. And it's the people—the bird hunters who cherish and respect the bobwhite. I like people who like quail. I have many reasons to love the little *"partridge."*

I no longer own bird dogs. I miss turning them loose for clients and for me, blowing the whistle "telling" them to roll on and to hunt farther out. I miss spotting them on a distant point, and handling the single or covey with style and manners, and finally, retrieving a dead bird to hand. The great quail days are etched in my mind.

I continue to hunt quail with great friends each season. Keith Burns and his family own a very nice South Texas ranch. The Burns' are "deer" people but they understand my affection for bobwhites and care-take their quail for me. Keith is a wonderful friend and is the kindest person I know.

I'd like to raise and train another liver and white pointer puppy, like Jasper, but I'm unsure if I ever will. One thing I do know for sure is that I'll continue to travel to great quail places. A covey rise of bobwhite quail over a stylish dog is my favorite and it's definitely…poetic.

The Boys

Georgia

August 31, 1999

Rachel, the boys, and I went to the Malone Pond. We fished from 7:15 – 8:20 P.M. It was a great evening. Newt came with us too. Cade caught 4 bass on a rubber worm, Cam caught 1 big bass, and I caught 2 on poppers. Rachel caught a really nice largemouth on the 5 weight...

By the time I was thirty-years-old, I hadn't settled down in one place since I finished college. I'd spent my twenties hunting in Canada's remotest corners, along the river breaks of the Yellowstone River in Montana, and in the bushveld of Zimbabwe. During those years, I lived out of small dome tents, plywood cabins, and safari camps. My existence was much like a wandering nomad. The only things I had to take care of were my rifles and shotguns, an old Ford truck, and a fine set of German-made binoculars.

The Boys

In this day and age, we find ourselves in different family settings as people come in and out of our lives. I became a stepdad to Cade and Camden and with their mom, moved to an 8,000 acre hunting preserve in Georgia. Their playground consisted of oak and pine forests, fields, creek bottoms, and ponds and an abundant supply of fish and wildlife. It was an idyllic setting and a paradise for Cade and Camden.

The boys were athletic, fast, and always had an endless supply of energy—they never stood still. They played T-ball, and then baseball, followed by flag football. We lived 12 miles from town, on a property with no immediate neighbors, and no other kids nearby. They had each other, fights were frequent enough, but nothing serious. They lived as brothers do, but in truth, they were inseparable best buddies. From the time Camden was a baby and muttered his first words, he called Cade: Bubba. And Cam still calls his brother Bubba to this day.

Our home was a simple, single story, white-brick dwelling shaded by towering oaks and pine trees. It stood at the end of a weaving dirt pathway, which was barely visible from the county road. When they weren't in school, Cade and Cam can spent most daylight hours outside. Georgia summers are sweltering and during those hot months, the boys were always shirtless, in shorts, and wore black rubber boots rather than sneakers. (I believe the boots just gave them the option to play not only in the dirt, but in the water and mud, too). I'd see them speed their bikes around our circular drive, then peddle hard and launch off a plywood jump to become temporarily airborne. They also raced through deep puddles that covered them with mud and water. They climbed trees, discovered poison ivy, played on parked tractors, and threw rocks and sticks at about everything. In the evenings, they'd come into the house with disheveled hair and bodies covered with a layer of dirt streaked with sweat. These wild boys knew how to keep themselves entertained.

As Cade and Cam grew a little older, they began to shoot BB guns. They knocked cans off fence posts and punched holes in paper targets; they quickly became marksman, and the odd quail that wandered into the yard was in grave danger and often bagged. The slain birds were always cleaned and eaten. Their appetite for adventure and their interest in the outdoors ensured they'd become skilled hunters. They also enjoyed fishing, and we all spent many late afternoons and evenings on the plantation's ponds that held bass and bream.

The smaller ponds were fished from the bank, and the larger ones were fished from our 13 foot fiberglass boat. Cade and Cam used their Zebco rods and caught fish on rubber worms. Our small Schnauzer, Newt, often came along, too as he loved to stand in the boat or walk in the shallows to chase minnows and frogs.

One evening, at dinnertime, I called out to the boys to come and eat. No reply. I called again. Nothing. I didn't see them anywhere in the nearby woods or in the deer food plot next to the house. A slight panic set in; the boys never played beyond sight of the house. Rachel and I rushed to the shed to check if they'd taken their bikes. The bikes were gone and so were their fishing rods. A fair distance behind the house, across a quail field, and beyond a woodlot was a large pond. We hoped that is where they went as the next closest fishing spot was much farther away. We left out of our yard and jogged along a winding path that cut through sorghum patches and stands of broom sedge. We called out to the boys as we hurried closer to the pond. Once in view of the water's edge, we saw Camden on the pond's dam—shirtless, in shorts, and rubber boots; he carried his rod in one hand and held the monofilament in the other with a two-pound largemouth flipping and flopping at the end of the line. With a big smile, he said, "Look Mama, I caught a bass!" Camden couldn't have been more than five at the time. Brother Cade was busy on the far bank, casting his purple rubber worm to rising fish along the edge of lily pads. That was the beginning of a lifetime affinity for fishing.

Hunting deer was a family affair, and from an early age, the boys accompanied us on most of those hunts. It was in Georgia that Cade killed his first deer—a big doe taken on a friend's property a few miles from our home. We lived on the plantation for five years. The boys were at home in the woods and on the water—they loved the outdoor life.

When Cade was ten and Cam was nine, our family moved to a South Texas ranch in the heart of the desolate brush country. Our boys had a new wilderness to explore.

The spring rains had been plentiful—the natural world responds well to moisture. The ranch was lush and green, and the ponds were to their highest levels. The locals told us that the deer, quail, wild hogs, cottontail, and jackrabbits were more abundant than any other time in recent history. (The rattlesnakes were as thick as fleas, too.) For two kids who loved to play and shoot, fish and hunt, our Texas ranch was a boyhood utopia. There was an endless supply of prey in all directions from the house, and the boys wasted no time to find it…and hunt it.

I wanted them to be responsible outdoorsmen and established a strict set of rules. First, whatever they killed had to be cleaned and eaten. Second, they were not to point or shoot each other with BB or pellet guns. (Many kids have lost their sight due to playful BB gun wars.) Third, if they saw a snake, they had to back away from it immediately and tell their mother or me about the sighting. I don't fret over snakes (except for black mambas), but I didn't want the boys to get anywhere close to rattlers—the ranch had big monstrous size ones with deadly venom.

As in Georgia, the boys played hard and routinely came home bruised, cut, bleeding, dirty, and wet. Cade and Cam always discovered creative ways to amuse themselves and were fearless when it came to exploring the ranch's almost impenetrable thorny thickets of mesquite, prickly pear cactus, and acacia. After school and on weekends, they spent daylight hours honing their hunting skills, stalking critters with their recurve bows and BB guns. Every so often, I'd drive up alongside them on a ranch road where they'd be walking side-by-side, carrying a weapon in one hand and a mixed-bag of cottontail rabbits and doves in the other. They were at home in the brush.

The Boys

Below our house, a short distance away, a deer feeder stood alongside a ranch road that cut through a large pasture of prairie grass. The feeder was an elevated 55 gallon drum that sprayed corn pellets in short bursts twice a day: once in the morning and again in the evening. The corn's primary purpose was to attract and feed deer, but it also filled the bellies of field mice, quail, doves, and wild hogs.

One scorching summer Saturday afternoon, about an hour before dark, the boys asked me for permission to sneak down to see if pigs were eating at the feeder. They wanted to shoot a hog if one was spotted. Wild hogs are among the most destructive and invasive animals in the country. In Texas, they are considered vermin. Wildlife authorities allow hunters and landowners to kill or capture them year-round and without any imposed limits. These feral pigs are shot from high-rack trucks, blinds, and helicopters; houndsmen release trained "hog" dogs to chase down and catch pigs. Wild hogs are unwelcome on most ranches and farms throughout the state. They are shot on sight.

I told them "Yes, go ahead, but be back by dark, and be careful." They carried recurve bows with low draw weights that shot arrows tipped with field points—equipment sufficient to kill a dove or rabbit, but with no chance of penetrating the tough hide of a feral pig, or so I thought. I didn't allow them to shoot broad heads, they were too young to handle razor-sharp blades.

It was nearly pitch black dark when they walked through the door and into the house.

"Did you see any pigs?" I asked

"Yeah, and I think we got one," Cam replied.

"What? You got one? You're joking right?" I quipped.

As the story goes, they approached the feeder and spotted six or seven pigs eating the scattered corn around the base of the feeder. They each nocked an arrow, crouched behind tall buffel grass and tumbleweed, and began to stalk and close the distance to the hogs. They stealthily crept to within 10 yards or so of the group of swine. Then, they drew back on their bows and each picked out a pig, aimed, and then let their arrows fly. Camden missed, but Cade didn't—he nailed one. The hog squealed, prompting the rest of the bunch to do the same and stampede into the nearby prairie of grass, kicking up dust and dirt as they bolted off. The squeals were heard until the pigs were out of sight.

Cam found his arrow, but Cade didn't. They looked for sign of the arrowed pig, but found no blood, hair, or any other evidence of a hit. There were tracks everywhere, making it almost impossible to tell where Cade's hog might have gone. It was getting dark, so they decided to head back home.

The boys told me they wanted to return to the feeder in the morning, and do all they could to find the pig. The animal was wounded, possibly dead, and needed to be found.

The following morning, soon after daybreak, Cade and Cam went out the door and headed to the feeder to look for the hog. I had ranch chores to do and told the boys I'd help them find the pig when I was through with my work. It was Sunday and the kids knew to be back to the house at a certain hour to get ready for church.

With my duties done, I made it back to the house, but the boys weren't back yet. Rachel hadn't heard from them. We assumed they

The Boys

found sign of the hog and were on its tracks. Time was getting tight to make the Sunday service at our small South Texas church, and the boys were still out wandering in the pasture.

Moments later, Camden burst into the house, out of breathe, and with sweat running down his face and neck.

"Gord, we got the pig, but it's not dead. We need a gun. Bubba is with the hog!"

"You can't be serious," I snapped.

I grabbed my .243 and a handful of cartridges, Cam and I went out the door, hopped into my Kawasaki Mule, and left out towards Cade and the pig. As I drove, Cam gave me a play-by-play of the morning's event.

They couldn't find any blood close by, so they decided to walk in the direction the pigs had run, hoping to find some blood or hair. As they walked, looking for trace of the hog, they spotted it under a *huisache* tree—a thorny drought-resistant acacia tree that provides shade in the South Texas summer heat. They managed to sneak up within bow range of the wounded pig, drew back, and released their arrows. Camden hit it this time, and Cade missed. The pig bolted into the grass. Like Kalahari bushmen, they followed the tracks in the dry dirt and waist-high buffel grass. There was little blood found, but they remained steady and kept going, following its tracks. Eventually, the pig slowed, they got close, and shot their arrows again. When they missed, their arrows were found in the grass. They kept after the hog. This sequence of events happened over and over until, finally, the pig had all their arrows in it and succumbed.

As soon as I saw Cade standing in the open prairie, I stepped harder on the throttle and sped towards him. Sure enough, there lay the pig, arrows sticking out everywhere—it was a ghastly sight. I handed the rifle to Cade, he carefully loaded a round in the chamber, walked a few steps closer to the hog, and shot it. It was over. They'd gotten their wild pig. It was too late for church service, it was already blazing hot and getting warmer by the minute, and we had a dead pig to deal with.

Overall, it was a messy ordeal—especially for the pig. As hunters, we must to do all we can to kill as quickly as possible. In hindsight, perhaps I made a poor decision to let them check the feeder with their underpowered bows and blunt field tips, but I always let the kids wander freely on the ranch. *Why stop now?* I thought.

With the prize pig laying on the flat bed of my Dodge ranch truck, we drove to the headquarters' game cleaning facility. We unloaded the pig, I took a few keepsake photos of the boys with their trophy. Cade and Cam gutted and cleaned the hog, and then hung it in the cooler. The boys did it on their own—from beginning to end.

They showed persistence and tirelessly searched for their wild hog. Once they found it, they showed skill and determination, the ability to track and finish the task they started. I was proud of them, they did it right.

––––––––––––

The boys started dove hunting once they were big enough to safely handle a 20 gauge shotgun. I remember taking Cade on

The Boys

his first dove outing. We stood under a mesquite tree on the edge of a sorghum field. He held his H & R single-shot 20 gauge, and anxiously waited for the white wing doves to fly in for their afternoon feeding. Soon enough, the birds arrived in droves; they swarmed in from every direction—it could have been easily mistaken for a high-volume dove shoot in Mexico or Argentina. Cade cocked the hammer back on his little shotgun and fired one round after another, and before he knew it, his game bag held the limit of 15 doves. He wore a grin from ear to ear.

Before long, Camden could shoot and handle a 20 gauge, and started dove hunting with his brother, mother, and me. One September afternoon, I recall seeing him, from across a planted sunflower field. He stood under a dark ebony tree, scanning the sky for incoming birds. He'd raise his double, shoot both barrels, and then run out from under the tree, shirtless; his skinny hips barely kept his shell pouch from dragging in the dirt. He'd pick up a fallen dove or two, and return to his lair under the tree. Cam didn't miss much.

For young hunters, their first buck is the biggest deal. It's a formative event, an achievement, a rite of passage. Every hunter remembers his first buck, it's a memory that lasts a lifetime.

The boys matured; they handled deer rifles with confidence and caution, and shot with precision. They'd successfully hunted whitetail does, wild pigs, and javalina. Camden once took a large bobcat at 264 paces—it was a heck of a shot.

I was with the boys when they took their first whitetail bucks. Cade, the older brother, killed his first, and Camden took his the following season. Both their bucks were taken on the Texas ranch where we lived, during those magical fleeting minutes as the sun dips down below the mesquite trees and brush. The boys were excited, eager, and nervous, but they killed their bucks with single, well-placed shots.

Their whitetail bucks were big and mature, but would be considered by most Texas ranch managers as management bucks, or perhaps as culls. But for me, their first bucks were great animals. I didn't care about the antler score, width, mass, or tine length— none of it mattered; they were trophies and I was proud of my boys. For every hunter, a first buck happens only once, and I was there for both of them.

When Cade was 14 and Cam was 13, they learned they were going to have a baby sister. The news wasn't received well, and we weren't surprised. Over the next few months, the boys began to warm to the idea of having a baby sister and looked forward to her arrival. The day Finley was born, her brothers immediately adored her. As a baby, Cade and Cam doted on Finley and were her endless source of entertainment. They gave her boundless attention and love, tickled and teased her, made goofy faces, and let her grip their fingers with her tiny hands. They always made her laugh and smile.

Today, the boys are young adults and live elsewhere. Finley sees her brothers only from time to time, and when she does, they give her love and attention, and they still make her laugh and smile. The bond between Finley and the boys remains strong, and I

The Boys

predict that will never change. From the day she was born, Finley has thought, and still thinks that Cade and Camden both hang the moon. They are wonderful brothers.

Years ago, I became a stepdad, and God blessed me to help raise two boys. I am so grateful.

Still Tracking

North Texas

January 3, 2016

.... I shot Brian's Franchi side-lock and my Parker 20 gauge. We hunted from 8:15 until 11:15. 30 quail—12 bobwhites and 18 blues. We saw 40 plus coveys. Goose did a great job retrieving birds. I shot better than I normally do. Awesome day. One of the best!

I am in awe whenever I walk the plains of North Texas, just below the Caprock, where great herds of buffalo once roamed and the Comanches hunted them. It's an expanse of badlands with mesas, buttes, and mottes of juniper and shinnery oak. Hackberries and cottonwoods border twisting, narrow creeks. Little bluestem, gramma, and broomweed grow, blanketing the flats. And there is quail in this country. In the good years, with abundant rainfall, there are gobs of them.

Still Tracking

My enduring affinity for days spent afield remains unchanged. I still need to crest the hill and see what is beyond the rise, and if nothing is discovered, I'll keep walking and searching. Great days are not measured solely by the shots fired, horns on the wall, or a filled game bag, but by the totality of the experience. It's about the comradery of friends, good laughter and easy talk, wild game, and the special places—both new haunts and familiar ones. And, for some, it's about contemplative silences. The urge to hunt is in my blood, and to hunt feels normal, like sleeping or eating. My fervor to chase game stems from the anticipation and the adventure. To kill is simply the fulfillment of the hunt. Nothing more.

The day after I graduated from college, I took a trail less traveled. I went hunting. I initially thought that my time in remote places was for a short while, but ultimately, it endured. One hunting season was followed by another and then another. My life in the outdoors continues to evolve. My passion became my vocation, which continues all these years later.

AUSTRALIA

August 7, 2016

This afternoon, we start flying back to Darwin and then on to Sydney. It's been a really great trip. Tommy and Ricky took very nice bulls and shot some old culls.

The weather was perfect. Simon is one of the hardest working PHs I know. We hunted in a true wilderness with lots of game. This might be the wildest place I've ever been....

I will hunt for the rest of my life, of this I'm certain. It affects me today no differently than it did when I was a kid. I once took a magnificent gemsbok bull after a long stalk on a high mountain in Namibia and the immediate sensibility I sensed once I held those long, black horns, reflectively carried me back to the November morning I killed my first deer in a hardwood draw in Quebec. Nothing has really changed.

I miss my bird dogs, life in the African bush, and many other places and things, too. But my grieved losses are replaced with new opportunity. My work allows me to travel and explore new whereabouts, carry a gun in unfamiliar territory, meet new people, and make new friends. It's an endless journey with few regrets.

There remain wild places where animals have never seen a man, and these places are, to me, of immense value. As hunters, we must continue to protect habitat, care for the animals we hunt and the ones we don't, and to always behave ethically. Sportsmen conserve and restore wildlife—it's been proven time and time again. Hunters are the stewards of game lands. This is an irrecusable fact.

My mother died in 1998. She was always loving and encouraging. My mother worried about me, and she was my biggest fan. Whenever I stopped in at my parent's home, after many months in Zimbabwe or some bush country in western Canada, my mother would ask me to tell her friends dramatic stories of marauding lions, charging elephants, and ferocious bears. Recounting stories

Still Tracking

embarrassed me and I shied away from disclosing any. Today, if I could, I'd tell her all the stories she might want to hear.

There was a time that I thought my best days had come and gone, but now I know that is untrue. I think about driven red grouse over heathery moors in England or Scotland, and I'm told they are especially fast, erratic in flight, and difficult to hit. The Lord Derby eland is an imposing antelope, and I hope, one day, to track a huge bull across the arid savannah of Cameroon. I look forward to the day that Finley sees her first wild elephant, which might be in the shadows of Mount Kilimanjaro or on the banks of the Zambezi River or somewhere else. It doesn't matter where she spots the elephant, I just want to be with her when she does. I want her to observe grizzly bears and wolves, an old buffalo bull and a big-maned lion, the Southern Cross and the Northern Lights. I want her to meet my friends in Argentina and spend time with a Masai girl her same age. Our natural world is vast, spectacular, and unpretentious. There is so much I want Finley to witness.

It's been almost twenty years since I shot my last ruffed grouse, but soon I'll travel with friends to the north woods of Maine to hunt them. I'll bring my journal and write about the hits and misses and the weather. And, if I'm lucky enough to take a grouse, I'll call my father and tell him, "Dad, I shot a *partridge* flying, just like an American!"

Acknowledgements

I'm especially grateful to Bill Pace, Berit Aagaard, and Craig Boddington. This book was written because you told me to do "something" with my field journals. Your support through this process is greatly appreciated.

To Frank Mullins, Mike Dorn, and Gayne Young. Thank you for your friendship and expertise. While any errors are the fault of the author, your insight and assistance was invaluable.

My experiences would not have been possible without the outfitters, ranchers, professional hunters, and business owners who hired me to guide their clients and work within their operations. I'm indebted to: Ross Elliott, Sam Borla, Sharon Borla, Dudley and Tess Rogers, David Morris, Chuck Larsen, Steve Spears, Bill Killmer, and Steve and Sally Grinnell. While they are deceased, I will always be indebted to Christian Payant and Scott Taylor.

I'm particularly grateful to all the clients I've guided over the years. With time shared in the field, clients become friends, and there are too many to list. You know who you are. Thank you.

A deep gratitude goes to Colonels Dennis and Loretta Behrens. You are not only wonderful business partners, but great friends and mentors. Words fall short to accurately express my sincerest thoughts and appreciation.

I cannot imagine a better editor and teacher than Mindy Reed of The Author's Assistant. This book would not have been possible without your guidance and encouragement. It has been a profound journey since our first meeting in that small coffee shop. Thank you Mindy!

And many thanks to Rebecca Byrd Arthur for the exceptional style and design of this book. The finished product exceeded my expectations.

Finally, to my caring and loving parents: Robert and Angele White. Your support and encouragement was unwavering and continues to this day. My heartfelt thanks.

About the Author

GORDIE WHITE was born and raised in Montreal, Canada. He grew up hunting and fishing with his father, brother, and grandfather. After completing a BA in Economics from Concordia University, Gordie began his big game guiding career. He has lived and hunted extensively throughout North America, Central America, South America, the South Pacific, and Africa. His professional pursuits include working in Zimbabwe with a safari company where he spent most of his time hunting elephant and buffalo. Stateside, he was the Operations Manager for a very successful hunting plantation in Georgia, and most recently, managed large hunting ranches in South Texas, dedicated to proper management for trophy whitetail deer and wild quail. Gordie has spent his professional career in the field, and now consults worldwide big game hunting and wing shooting. He lives with his daughter in Wimberley, Texas.

CPSIA information can be obtained
at www.ICGtesting.com
Printed in the USA
FSOW03n0048060118
42925FS